The Authentic Attorney:
The Winning Psychology of Great Trial Lawyers

by
Stephen A. Hnat
With Ven Johnson, Esq.

The contents of this work, including, but not limited to, the accuracy of events, people, and places depicted; opinions expressed; permission to use previously published materials included; and any advice given or actions advocated are solely the responsibility of the author, who assumes all liability for said work and indemnifies the publisher against any claims stemming from publication of the work.

All Rights Reserved
Copyright © 2022 by Stephen A. Hnat

No part of this book may be reproduced or transmitted, downloaded, distributed, reverse engineered, or stored in or introduced into any information storage and retrieval system, in any form or by any means, including photocopying and recording, whether electronic or mechanical, now known or hereinafter invented without permission in writing from the publisher.

Dorrance Publishing Co
585 Alpha Drive
Suite 103
Pittsburgh, PA 15238
Visit our website at www.dorrancebookstore.com

ISBN: 979-8-8868-3127-6
eISBN: 979-8-8868-3986-9

The Authentic Attorney:
The Winning Psychology of Great Trial Lawyers

by
Stephen A. Hnat
With Ven Johnson, Esq.

Dedication

There are many people who contributed to the lessons I have tried to communicate in this book. I have a special sense of gratitude to Geoffrey Nels Fieger, Ven Johnson, and Gerry Spence for the opportunities, lessons, and friendships they have so generously given me. Their courage and compassion in the practice of law are an inspiration. I am also grateful to William McHenry, Jeff Stewart, Craig Hilborn, and many other attorneys who have shared their insight, friendship, and support with me. I have learned from too many trial attorneys to mention but not too many to appreciate and love. Above all, this book is dedicated to my personal heroes, my sons Anthony and Vincent, who have dedicated their lives to the armed services, fighting for the liberties implicit in the pages of this book. If there is one phrase that envelops all of these people, it is "Semper Fidelis." Thank you all for your meaning and love.

A Forward by Geoffrey Fieger

Steve Hnat and I were young together once. It was back in the late eighties when our paths first crossed in Ann Arbor, Michigan. I was an ambitious young lawyer who wanted, someday, to be a real trial lawyer like my hero Gerry Spence. Sure, I would soon go on to win several multimillion dollar cases... but I was far from a household name, even in Michigan, my own backyard.

Back then, Steve was a renowned psychotherapist. He had made a name for himself by advising and treating the Detroit professional sports teams and their athletes about drug issues.

I remember liking Steve as soon as I met him. He has an ingratiating personality. He looks at you directly in the eye with inviting manner that puts you at ease. We hit it off immediately.

Over the next few years I would occasionally refer clients to Steve and bounce ideas off him for my upcoming trials. I remember telling him more than once that he would make a damn fine jury consultant. He would just laugh and tell me that he enjoyed being a therapist. After all, he had a stable job, in a great community. He was earning quite a name for himself. And, he had a wife and 5 kids to support.

The nineties were a whir for me. I began representing Dr. Jack Kevorkian in all those assisted suicide murder cases, while simultaneously trying to keep a lid on an exploding civil practice that was expanding nationally. Steve was never far from my thoughts, and I would regularly consult with him about my trials.

By 1998, I had become a household name in my own backyard. Rather impulsively I declared my candidacy for the Democratic nomination for Governor the State of Michigan. I had never run for a political office before. I knew nothing about politics. I was a complete amateur. But I did one thing right. I asked Steve

Hnat to take a short sabbatical to be my speech writer. I had a feeling he could write in my voice. I was right.

I won the nomination quite handily by beating two well-known party hacks in the primary. The Democratic party wasn't too happy about that, and walked away from me in the general election. Steve and I would often joke that the assassin had come uninvited to their party.

My political experience left me more convinced than ever that my life's calling was as a trial lawyer. Politics made me feel dirty. Pursuing justice for my clients made me feel free and clean. But I knew I couldn't do it without my pal. Steve had become my voice.

When I really want something, I can be very convincing, and I really wanted Steve to become my full-time jury and trial consultant. I finally convinced him, and for the last 30 years, more or less, we have been together, a team.

Steve and I have withstood the onslaught of hundreds of trials in more than half the states in the country. We have faced the good, bad, and ugly. Great judges. Biased judges. Capable insurance counsel. Arrogant, blowhard insurance hacks. Through it all, more or less, we have come through victorious.

Steve understands people. He understands the need for trial lawyers to tell a succinct and compelling story. Steve understands how juries coalesce around leaders, and more importantly, who the leaders are. Most of all, Steve understands me. I could not have done what I have done without him.

This book sets forth the essential tools that every trial lawyer should bring to the table. While the phrase "must read" is over wrought, anyone aspiring to be a real trial lawyer would be well advised to take this book to heart. Knowing Steve, the heart is exactly where it came from.

Geoffrey Fieger
Geoffrey Fieger has won more multi-million-dollar verdicts and settlements than any attorney in history.

Introduction

About twenty-five years ago, I was a psychologist with a successful therapy practice in Ann Arbor, Michigan, when I met a local trial attorney struggling with a case he was working on. The attorney represented a patient who had suffered permanent brain damage after a psychiatrist had improperly administered a neuroleptic drug. The attorney wasn't sure how to best present his evidence to a jury.

I'd studied neuropharmacology, so I helped the attorney understand what happened to his client in a way that he found useful in preparing his case. I didn't know it at that time, but he was showing a characteristic that would later make him one of the most successful trial attorneys of our generation: a willingness to understand and communicate how the damage done to his client affected her instead of just reporting the damages to a jury. The attorney, Geoffrey Fieger, had just passed his bar exam, and this was a first-of-its-kind lawsuit. He'd never argued a case in a jury trial before, but he went on to win a verdict of over one million dollars in the case.

We became friends, and from time to time, he'd call to talk about his cases. Increasingly, we found ourselves talking about how jurors react to evidence and the way it's presented by attorneys. We talked about how juries relate to an attorney and how some attorneys came across as sincere and trustworthy while others seemed manipulative or unfeeling. He intuitively understood that his credibility with jurors was key to his success. He was right.

In another case, Geoff represented a woman who was suing her gynecologist for a botched procedure. The plaintiff had been mutilated by the doctor's laser procedure for vaginismus, and Fieger wondered if he should show the jury photos of the damage. The images were graphic and disturbing. They showed the physical

1

damage done to her. Although he was primarily concerned that showing the pictures might offend some of the four men and four women on the jury, the psychologist in me was struck by how the mutilated genitals might affect his client emotionally. We began a discussion that I have since repeated countless times with other attorneys on how important it was to communicate how damages *affect the client* and how to communicate this to a jury. "How are they going to react to these pictures?" Geoff asked. "Are these images going to help her case or hurt it?" I glanced again at the photos. They were pretty gruesome.

"The male jurors will see these and give you whatever you ask for," I told him, handing the pictures back. "The women will look at them differently, though." The comment about men might have been insensitive or dismissive, but I was more immediately drawn to understanding how the client experienced the injury and how other women might understand it.

I felt the women on the jury needed to see the pictures in the right context. I knew about the "golden rule" (never ask jurors to put themselves in the client's place), so we discussed how to create the right *context* for sharing the photos with the jury. "Invite jurors to put themselves in situations they might share in common with your client," I said. "How would they feel if they were her?"

Geoff thought about this for a while. His client's pain and mutilation would be hidden to most by her clothing. But how would she feel in her most intimate moments, her most vulnerable moments? How would she feel on her wedding night, or the first time with her lover?

"These scars ... these injuries that seem so private to the world are never private to her," Geoff said. "They are a constant source of pain to her emotionally and will affect her for the rest of her life. Those times that should be a source of joy in her life will become a source of suffering instead. The first time she is going to make love to her partner ... maybe on her wedding night ... a time that should be exciting, passionate, and joyful will be filled with terror and apprehension. Embarrassment. Humiliation. This will always be with her. This is what she'll have to live with."

Fieger's thoughts would make their way into and help shape his closing argument. Putting his client's damages in the context of an experience that is familiar to jurors helped them to understand the real impact on her life. As Geoff addressed the jury, it was clear to me and the jury that he genuinely understood his client's pain. He felt for her. He cared enough to feel for her. The idea of a male attorney understanding the emotional impact of this type of injury might have seemed presumptuous, but Geoff conveyed compassion the jury could feel and share. The verdict was over twenty-five million dollars, most of it for non-economic damages.

Since those early years, I've made a career out of helping plaintiff attorneys prepare and present their cases in court. I've worked on nearly two hundred jury trials which combined resulted in over a billion dollars in jury verdicts. I've worked with some of the best personal injury attorneys in the profession, studying their techniques, learning from their success, and coaching them on techniques that help them connect with jurors and present compelling evidence in a way that resonates in a courtroom. I'm typically involved in a trial from the start, sitting at the plaintiff's table and advising attorneys about how to present their cases while paying close attention to how and why jurors are reacting.

This vantage point has given me a rare perspective on the jury trial process. As a trained and experienced psychologist and therapist, I have the luxury of watching juries form and take shape, from voir dire to closing statements and post-trial jury interviews, and this has allowed me to develop a set of principles and methods that time and again have helped attorneys win their cases with large damage verdicts.

Honing Your Skills

This book is for any attorney who wants to perform better in the courtroom. It will help you select receptive juries and deliver messages that help your client and build support from jurors and even judges. Veteran attorneys will also find value in reading about these principles and methods, but younger attorneys who've been in practice for ten years or fewer and have scant trial experience will likely benefit the most.

I recently sat in on some training sessions a stellar trial attorney was giving advice to some of the younger associates in his office. He met with these associates two at a time to talk about their cases and upcoming trials. These associates were all smart people and good lawyers, but when it came to trial preparation, they had a lot to learn. Law school had trained them to understand the *mechanics* of trials but had done little to help these lawyers understand the *psychology* behind selecting jurors and presenting a case. He struggled to shift their focus from the technical content to the process- how to prepare their case to persuade a jury.

Young attorneys coming out of law school see cases from a technical perspective. They see trials in terms of motions in law, rulings and rules, and court procedures. They understand the value of expert witnesses, careful questioning, and presenting evidence in a logical and concise order. It's a normal effect of the type of education they receive but often leaves them unprepared to be successful.

What they often don't understand is how to tell a compelling story to provide a narrative that makes their case clear-cut and indisputable. They don't understand how to spot biases in the jury pool or how to draw those biases out in a way that helps their case. They don't understand the importance of confronting their own biases and being authentic and vulnerable before a jury. They don't understand how crucial it is to find the *meaning* of their case and convey that perspective in a way that convinces jurors to take up their cause.

Trials are about justice, and they involve humans who have been hurt. But many young attorneys never develop a sense of the meaning of justice in a case or the compassion for the suffering client or learn how to effectively exhibit empathy in court. They often don't understand that compassion has to be the foundation for how they approach their work because that ultimately is what will persuade a jury. This book will help you develop or refine those skills in a way that will dramatically increase your chances of winning.

The Courage to Be Honest

We will talk a lot in this book about the importance of being authentic. This is something else many attorneys struggle with in the courtroom. They are self-conscious or insecure about being open and caring, and they either find themselves showing no sense of humanity or their empathy comes across as forced or fake. They imitate other attorneys, try out "tricks" they learned from seminars (or books), or perform the way an attorney might on a TV show. They try to seduce jurors rather than communicate with them, and that often comes across as insincere or even deceitful. The legal field tends to attract people who prefer to be more intellectual and rational in their thinking, but successful plaintiff attorneys understand they need to go beyond that. They need to be willing to confront their own prejudices and have the courage and confidence to be honest and open in front of a jury.

Trials are more than a legal process. They are a social process and a healing process. Recognizing these dynamics will increase your effectiveness in trials because it requires you to develop your emotional acuity and interpersonal skills. Understanding more about yourself will boost your ability to understand your client and jurors. Ultimately, this understanding is the foundation of compassion, enlightenment, and, above all, justice.

Winning cases is one thing, but finding great satisfaction in your work is critical, too. Some of the unhappiest people I've ever met have been financially successful trial attorneys. They've made a fortune doing trials, but they're miserable because they don't have the sense that what they are doing is meaningful. It's another case, another win, more money, and perhaps more fame. Happiness doesn't necessarily flow from their success.

Following the blueprint I've drawn up in this book helps with that as well. A lot of the meaning we have in life comes from knowing that we've helped someone who's been wronged or injured. Someone needed us, and we came through for them in an open and honest way. For most people, there is no greater satisfaction in life than feeling this way. If you feel good about the work you're doing, you're going to feel good about yourself. If this book helps you define your success in this way, then I will have done my job. This book will help you be a better lawyer, but it will also help you be a better human being.

What You'll Learn

The science of persuasion has been well-established for many years but is rarely brought up in books and workshops for trial attorneys. We're going to change that. This book will provide you with a roadmap to help you get from jury selection to closing argument with a coherent and consistent plan. Here are some of the other things we'll talk about:

Voir dire: Trial attorneys understand that voir dire is crucial to winning, but most don't prepare adequately for it. They fail to confront their own biases about an issue or their client, and they rarely develop a plan for coaxing jurors to reveal their own prejudices. Voir dire is not entirely about eliminating biased jurors; it's crucial to establish your credibility and honesty with jurors—qualities that will support your case throughout the trial.

Opening statements: Opening statements are more than an outline for the case you're about to present. Rather, they provide a cognitive framework for helping jurors understand the evidence—a mental Rosetta Stone for jurors that defines the evidence as the glass half empty or half full depending on how you want them to understand it.

Preparing a witness: This does not mean scripting or rehearsing a witness. That only diminishes their credibility and effectiveness. The best preparation is when you help your witnesses understand the significance of their evidence to the essential narrative of a case, enabling them to testify concisely and coherently.

Damages: An effective presentation of damages can lead to big verdicts and drive other verdicts, such as negligence. But it's equally important to view this portion of the trial as part of your client's healing. When we tell our client's story and convince the jury to take up their cause, victims heal more completely.

In an overarching sense, this book will help you get out of your head and into your heart. You will learn how to use introspection to better understand the obstacles that you, as well as a jury pool, might face in trying to appreciate the true meaning of your case. There is a science to persuasion and a science to winning personal injury cases. But there is also a lot of humanity involved, and the best attorneys understand this and know how to integrate strategy and compassion in a way that helps victims heal and encourages jurors to play a key role in the story you're crafting.

How I Got Here

On a sunny Saturday morning years ago, I got another call from Geoff Fieger. He asked if I would meet with a potential client. "I think the guy might be crazy, but I don't know," Geoff said. "Can you talk to him and tell me what you think?"

The client's name was Dr. Jack Kervorkian, the Michigan pathologist who was at the center of the national assisted suicide debate. Starting in 1990, he had assisted in about 130 suicides, often using a self-made suicide machine he called either his Mercitron or the Thanatron. He had a flamboyant public persona, often dressing in tattered clothes he purchased from the Salvation Army, and once appeared in court wearing colonial garb to protest the antiquated charges he faced. His friends described him as witty and good-natured, but those who met him in social situations portrayed him as awkward, unpredictable, and quick to anger. He seemed to like all the publicity he received.

I didn't think Kervorkian was crazy, but after meeting with him, I concluded he was eccentric and death-phobic. He had immigrated to the U.S. with his mother and sister to flee genocide in Armenia, and he knew many people who had been killed in the mass executions and death marches into the Syrian desert. One of his relatives died soon after arriving in the U.S., and at one point, the family dog died in Kervorkian's arms. He grew up to become a pathologist, studied how people died, and his agreement a with his assisted suicide patientswas that he would help them die if they allowed him to measure their pupils as they expired. He literally stared into their eyes as they died. His whole life was centered on understanding the process of death, and I felt this was his way of dealing with the prospect of his own passing.

Fieger took Kervorkian on as a client, and I came to work in Geoff's office as a "trial consultant". Understand that we did not expect a big payday; Kervorkian had no money to pay legal fees, and he freely admitted doing what he'd been charged with. There was a high likelihood that we would lose. However, we saw this case as a way to change social policy and help relieve the suffering of many people. So we presented the case as a civil rights issue. People should have a choice on how they die, we argued. Their decision is based on their own conscience with input from loved ones and family. We emphasized the compassion and mercy that Kervorkian showed his patients. We identified a very different meaning to the case than the prosecutors, and it was a meaning that the juries understood.

The strategy worked. From May 1994 to June 1997, Kervorkian stood trial for homicide four times. We won three acquittals, and the fourth ended in a mistrial. Kervorkian ultimately rode his success at trial to fame and fortune, but if you were a casual observer, you'd think he was indifferent to all that. In fact, he spent the time in trial teaching himself Japanese, barely paying attention to the testimony and legal arguments.

Then in 1999, after *60 Minutes* broadcast a tape showing Jack helping a patient die by giving him a lethal injection, Kervorkian was charged with first-degree murder. He ignored Geoff's advice and decided to represent himself at trial. I was happy to no longer be involved. In my mind, the doctor had gone too far with the *60 Minutes* tape, and I felt Kervorkian had lost focus on the purpose of his actions. His case was supposed to be about compassion, free will, and civil rights, but Kervorkian made it impossible for jurors to support abstract principles when they were confronted with the raw footage showing someone dying by lethal injection at the hand of the plaintiff. Kervorkian lost and went to prison for eight years.

Other Cases Beckoned

I would go on to work with Geoff Fieger and many other attorneys in the next several decades. I came to see the legal process as a way to affect social policy as well as help heal individuals involved in the trials. In one of our first cases, we represented a homeless, black veteran named Edward Swans. As a disabled veteran myself, his case seemed particularly tragic to me. Swans had been honorably discharged from the military with a service-related disability of schizophrenia, and though he functioned well when on medication, he often wound up hospitalized at the local VA facility.

Swans wandered the streets of Lansing, Michigan, and one winter day in 1996 when it was twenty-seven degrees below zero, he walked into the police station and announced that he had been assaulted. He was not wearing a shirt, coat, or socks and had icicles in his beard, but the cops knew he was schizophrenic and put him back out on the street. Swans then went to what he thought was a halfway house he'd lived in once and began banging on the door with a broom. But it wasn't a halfway house; it was a daycare center, and the people inside called the police, thinking Swans was breaking the door down with an ax.

Instead of treating Swans as a chronic schizophrenic and taking him to the hospital for treatment, police took him back to the station. During booking, Swans became uncooperative, and the police slammed him to the floor and forcefully hog-tied him in a device known as a kick-stop restraint, which fastens someone's arms and legs to a waist strap. Prisoners should never be held face-down when in a kick-stop restraint, but that's exactly what these Lansing officers did. One doctor who reviewed the case said the behavior of the police amounted to "group-oriented torture." The video of the scene showed a puddle of urine forming as Swan died face down on the floor with six cops applying pressure to his wrist, chin, shoulders, ear, and nose.

No one would take the case, but Fieger and I eventually found a relative and filed a lawsuit on Swans' behalf. We were getting destroyed in the media because the police were seen as heroes who'd saved the daycare from a dangerous, deranged individual. In the courtroom, we told a different story. We felt Swans had been the victim of excessive force and that his constitutional rights to medical and psychological care had been violated. The police had lied about how they killed Swans, and we felt strongly that they shouldn't be allowed to get away with that. The trial lasted twenty-seven days, and the all-white jury heard from more than thirty witnesses. After deliberating for two days, jurors returned a verdict in favor of Swans's estate in the amount of nine point eight million dollars.

These high-profile cases were about causes as much as clients, and they helped me clearly see what sets successful attorneys apart. Whether they are stars like Gerry Spence or Ven Johnson on the plaintiff's side or stars like Mark Zausmer on the defense side, they all display immense courage. In the face of death threats, hostile media, or financial risks, they never lose focus. They never lose their humanity.

My role has evolved over the years, and now I consult with a variety of attorneys. I like to get involved with their cases at the very start. I help the attorney think through the story they're going to tell, how they're going to present it, and what expert testimony they'll need. I help with pretrial research if the case calls for it, and I sit with the attorney through voir dire, sharing my thoughts on what questions to ask, which jurors we should keep, and which ones we should try to keep off the jury. Sometimes I help write the opening statement and the closing argument. Through it all, I read the jury, gauging their reactions and advising the attorneys on how they can better drive home the meaning of the case they are arguing.

What This Book Is and What It Isn't

You'll find this book is unlike most books on doing trial work. Those books are written by trial lawyers, and they'll tell you how to successfully conduct a case. How do you conduct discovery? How do you prepare witnesses? How do you prepare for pretrial conferences and preliminary hearings?

This book is different. It's less about the physical preparations involved in civil jury trials and more about the mental preparations lawyers must make. In many ways, it's an extended argument in support of using honesty and veracity in a courtroom, even when that approach runs counter to what we often see in trials across the country. I'm a psychologist and not an attorney, and my expertise is in reading people and helping others look inside themselves to find the integrity and candor they need to win over a jury. That is not always an easy ask for trial attorneys. Many are known for their theatrics and flair for drama. But after twenty-five years of developing cases, working with some of the most skilled lawyers of my generation and closely watching the ebb and flow of scores of high-profile trials, I know that being authentic is the only sure path to victory with a jury.

Much of what I share in this book I learned from others. I've had the advantage of seeing the "rabbit pulled from the hat" in many trials, and I've also been lucky enough to be in a position while sitting next to the attorney to learn *why* that rabbit-in-the-hat trick worked so well. I listen, observe, and ask questions. It's been a journey to understanding, and now I want to take you on this journey.

Whenever I work with an attorney on a case, I counsel two things at the onset. First, whatever you are doing that works for you, continue doing it. Psychology is a science and you can use that science to your advantage in a trial. But some attorneys also have powerful instincts, and you should never question your intuition if that strategy helps you win in court.

My second piece of advice is to always try to deepen your understanding of how your approach works and why it works for you. This self-reflection improves your effectiveness and translates to other trial skills because it fortifies your confidence as well as your vulnerability, both of which are key elements in connecting with a jury.

While the principles of persuasion are well-established and constant across cultures, the most effective application of those principles depends on the attorney adapting them to their own personality. Be yourself always. A good attorney makes these techniques their own and becomes comfortable using them. You must be yourself in front of a jury, as role-playing another attorney or their style inevitably fails. You must adapt, not adopt, these principles and techniques.

The following chapters will offer strategic and tactical suggestions and examples of how to apply them to trial work. There will also be discussions of the theory explaining why these techniques work, and examples of how other attorneys have adapted and used the techniques. All of this will provide you with enough understanding to allow you to modify the techniques to your own style and comfort level.

This material may seem elementary to seasoned trial attorneys, but I encourage even veteran litigators to take it to heart. Sometimes we develop bad habits and approach trial preparation in a rote manner. Every trial attorney has an aspect of their technique they feel should improve, and this book should help give you a fresh perspective. I've seen some great trial attorneys experience an epiphany when they have successfully adopted some of the principles I describe in this book.

My Focus on Plaintiffs

Finally, a word for my defense bar friends. I work primarily for plaintiffs because it fits with my training as a psychotherapist focused on helping those who suffer. The Kervorkian and Swans trials helped me appreciate how trials bring justice and social progress, but also how they help victims of injustice heal. This book takes the plaintiff's perspective because I am most knowledgeable and comfortable speaking from that point of view.

The defense bar is just as essential and meaningful, but some of the specific considerations are different and the civil trial goals are somewhat different. Nevertheless, the techniques outlined in this book are just as effective for defense attorneys. What's more, the theoretical foundations outlined in this book will not only improve your effectiveness as an attorney, they will also improve your life. Authenticity, compassion, and making a difference in people's lives always lead to personal growth and fulfillment.

I've heard many attorneys over the decades say they only want to hear what works and not necessarily *why* it works. That is shortsighted. They'll attend seminars and read books written by legal rock stars and sometimes they pick up a "trick" or two. But more often than not, they experience the futility of imitating another attorney's style and never develop a true and honest style of their own. Effectively adapting techniques requires a personal understanding of how those techniques will work for you.

Jury trials are as much a social process as they are a legal process. The same qualities that create successful social skills apply during a jury trial. When meeting people at a social event, we are drawn to authentic people and repelled by phonies.

Jurors begin trials as skeptics, and they are especially skeptical of the plaintiff's attorney. He's the "ambulance chaser" or the "TV lawyer" they see in commercials and on billboards. Jurors expect the plaintiff's attorney to be in it for one reason: a big payday. This is a tough hurdle to clear, and being honest and forthright with jurors is the only way to earn the trust and credibility necessary to win trials. Your jurors' decision on whether to adopt your interpretation of the evidence is based on a simple perception. Are you "for real"? Do you truly care about the client and getting justice for them, or are do you only care about the money?

Whether we like it or not, jury verdicts are based on the jurors' understanding of the evidence and not your interpretation of the evidence. I can't tell you how many times attorneys I know were certain the proofs cemented their case only to have juries use the same evidence to support the other side! Evidence is like a glass half empty or half full. Each person will see it differently. Most verdicts are based on which attorney the jury trusted most. Attorneys must earn that trust and credibility through their authenticity, and the only way to ensure you project that genuineness is by honing your emotional acuity and interpersonal skills. Understanding more about yourself will increase your ability to understand your client and jurors. Ultimately, this understanding is the foundation of compassion, enlightenment, and justice.

Chapter One:

The Science of Persuasion

Ven Johnson had worked as a defense attorney successfully for nearly a decade when he "switched sides" and became a plaintiff attorney. When I started working with him, he was still relatively new to this type of work, and his behavior in the courtroom showed this. It's a difficult transition. It requires a different perspective and calls for a different preparation.

In one of his early trials, Ven put a witness on the stand in a wrongful death case. The witness had lost a family member, and while he started out testifying in a calm voice, he soon became more emotional as he talked about the brother he lost. But the moment the witness's voice cracked or he paused to collect himself, Ven would jump in and quickly change the subject. It was almost as if he didn't want his witness to show any emotion on the stand.

At a break, I asked him about this tactic. "Why are you steering the witness away from the emotion he's feeling? Why don't you let him feel it and cry?" I asked. "What are you talking about? I feel bad for him!" "The jury needs to feel what the witness is feeling," I said. "That's the only way you can win this case!" "Bullshit," Johnson said, getting angry. "I let this guy cry on the stand, and the jury is going to think I'm just milking the situation! They're going to be offended and think I am manipulating his grief."

I took a deep breath. "You're thinking like a defense attorney still," I said. "You have to drive into that emotion. It's honest, and it's true. You've got to let that hurt show. It's the only way the jury will feel it and truly understand it. And you have to let yourself show that hurt for him."

Ven is one of the most compassionate men I know, and what I didn't understand at the time is that he was trying to protect his client from feeling that pain. Ven didn't want to feel that he was being an instrument of the client's pain. He didn't have to learn how to change from a defense attorney to a plaintiff attorney as much as he needed to learn how to use his own emotions to communicate.

Over the course of the trial, though, Ven came to see the value of what I was telling him, and in time, he became as brilliant as a plaintiff's attorney as he had been a defense lawyer. He did this by putting in the work, the work of examining his own biases and discomfort about emotional testimony, and the work of learning how to bring that emotion out before a jury in a sincere, genuine way.

What Johnson and all great lawyers come to understand is that emotions play a key role in trials, because emotion plays a key role in how all of us, including jurors, make decisions. If you want jurors to understand your client's perspective, they must be engaged and impassioned by what they hear and see in the courtroom. As the great poet Maya Angelou once said, "People will forget what you said, people will forget what you did, but people will never forget how you made them feel."

Subjectively and consciously, we all get a certain feeling about a person or situation, and that perceptual-emotional prism shapes our subsequent beliefs and actions. This process happens in fractions of seconds, and our first conscious experience of emotion happens only at the end of this process. The process is predictable, biological, and inescapable, and the implications for how it affects human understanding and behavior are profound.

Lawyers who understand this have an edge in the courtroom. They are able to get jurors emotionally involved and moved by the plaintiff's story. Jurors feel it, identify with it, and are affected by it. The attorney whose case speaks to jurors on an emotional level is almost assured of winning. Emotion has a central, irrevocable power to influence our decisions. If you want to persuade a jury to accept your version of an event, you have to help them understand and truly "feel" your client's pain.

The Science Involved

Our understanding of the cognitive sciences and neurobiology have increased significantly in recent years, and these two fields have converged on a common understanding of the fundamental role brain activity and emotion play in shaping human perception and behaviors. The brain uses emotional information processing to organize, understand, and respond. Long before we have a conscious thought, our brain has already begun to organize perceptions and label them with emotions. This reduces the time it takes to understand and act on what is happening.

For example, imagine two of our ancient ancestors making their way across the savanna. One of the hunters notices that some birds off in the distance suddenly start cackling loudly and that some small wild mammals are scurrying away from the same general area. He immediately senses danger and runs. This is emotional, or affective, information processing, and it exerts a powerful effect on perceptions and decisions.

His companion, meanwhile, also notices the cackling. He stops. "Something has changed," he thinks. Wildlife is scurrying away from the same area. What's going on? He scans the horizon and notices the tall grass is moving suspiciously. What's that? Is it related to the cackling birds, the scurrying wildlife? Then he spies a large brown figure emerge, and he thinks, "It's a lion! Lions eat people and this one is coming my way!" He turns and flees, but he's too late to outrun the lion. This is logical information processing, and if all our ancient ancestors thought this way, our species may not have made it out of the prehistoric period.

We have evolved to respond to and evaluate information affectively first and logically later; it's the only way we can survive. Both hunters' initial perceptions evoked a sense that something had changed in the environment. Both focused on those changes and both made the same ultimate decision- run like hell. But the first hunter survived because he relied on his emotions to act more quickly. He didn't *understand* his perceptions (cackling birds, frightened wildlife), but his *emotional response* to those perceptions saved his life. Today, we don't typically find ourselves running from lions, but we nevertheless have "gut reactions," "instincts," or a "sixth sense" that influences our decision-making.

Neuroradiological studies using P.E.T. scans reveal that we recall the emotions of memory before we recall the logical content of that memory. That's because our perceptions are routed through areas of the brain that evaluate and label perceptions in an emotional context. Neuroscientists have found that people whose brains are damaged in the area that generates emotions are incapable of making decisions.

This process of recalling emotions before an actual memory is called transference, and psychotherapists use these emotional reactions to identify past traumas their patients can't remember but which are still affecting their present behavior. In effect, the traumatic emotions of the past are transferred to a present circumstance. We get a feeling about someone or a situation, and emotional transference prompts us to see it through a perceptual-emotional prism.

Why is any of this useful to a plaintiff's attorney preparing for a jury trial? Because it helps to explain why minimizing emotional testimony and emphasizing logical explanations, something many attorneys are by nature inclined to do, doesn't necessarily help their case. Our species, and our juries by extention, have evolved to initially respond to and evaluate information affectively first and logically later. Emotions cue action. Emotions trigger changes in behavior. Logic, on the other hand, cues learning and lulls us into a passive understanding.

A courtroom, in this sense, is not a classroom. Trials are not designed to be an educational experience. Trials are designed to evoke emotion, compel action, and persuade others to see the same view of the world that you, the plaintiff's attorney, see. Using emotion is the fastest and surest route to that outcome.

First Impressions

That said, the role emotions play in trials is far subtler than many understand. As perceptions flood into his brain during a trial, a juror's mind unconsciously evaluates and labels these perceptions with emotions. Those emotional labels then exert a powerful priming influence on the juror's subsequent behavior. Unconscious emotional reactions shape our understanding and reactions to an experience before we are aware of either the emotions or the reactions.

Jurors go through this process in response to you and your arguments. You may not even be aware of your own emotions about the matter, but jurors will perceive them and respond with emotional reactions of their own. In the case that Ven Johnson was presenting at the beginning of this chapter, his own discomfort with emotional testimony was making it difficult for jurors to experience the powerful sense of loss and pain being conveyed by the witness.

What's more, jurors decide who they trust and consider to be credible through emotional information processing. First impressions are an emotional reaction, and those first impressions are usually determinative. It's profoundly difficult to overcome a bad first impression in the short span of a jury trial. Jurors react to what you say and do long before you or they realize it, and as a result, they often choose sides early and establish a powerful preference for who they will trust and believe as the trial goes on.

This is not to say that jurors are not affected by the evidence presented later. But their first impression *will* shape how they hear and understand that evidence. This is why authenticity is an essential quality for any trial attorney. What you believe and what you feel are in plain sight, and there is nowhere for you to hide or disguise yourself. I've seen some attorneys successfully cast a false impression, but the effect is very short-term. Veteran trial attorney John Secrest called these deceptive practitioners "two-day lawyers" because that is about how long they can maintain the façade before it cracks and juries see the lawyer for who he truly is. All trust is lost at that point.

The beauty of the jury system is that its decisions are collective. You might be able to fool one or two jurors, but it's nearly impossible to hoodwink the entire jury. The diversity of juror experience and perceptions makes a jury more reliable than a polygraph because of their built-in resistance to manipulation. If you are honest and forthright, jurors will see that and trust you. They may not understand the evidence, but they understand who they can trust and they will trust what you present to them. By the same token, they won't believe *anything* from an untrustworthy lawyer.

Being authentic sounds easy, and it can be. But often it requires that you become aware of your own biases and obstacles the way Ven Johnson did on his way to becoming a stellar plaintiff's attorney. Authenticity requires more than merely "telling the truth"; you have to be aware of your own emotions and how you are expressing them, and that requires an accomplished level of emotional intelligence. Jurors clearly see the characters in the drama that is played out before them. They know who is real and who is fake, and in my experiences talking with jurors after scores of trials, I can tell you that they are nearly always accurate. They see you. If you want to communicate with them and persuade them, you must have a finely honed self-awareness and emotional acuity.

What It Takes

Great trial attorneys are often described as having good instincts with people. They have a knack for communicating directly and openly. They put people at ease, and there is nothing forced or false-toned about the emotions they express. Often, this persona comes naturally to them, but others I've worked with have had to work hard to cultivate this natural warmth and honesty. The work involves a certain amount of introspection and honesty to themselves. They come to understand their greatest fears and how to keep those fears in perspective, and this gives them an air of confidence and vulnerability that resonates with jurors.

Great attorneys are not born with good emotional instincts, but they've learned to recognize what they feel and what others feel and act accordingly. There is a bit of trial and error involved, but in time, they learn to trust their instincts and to use those instincts to persuade. This helps them win trials, of course, but it also leads them to a more meaningful life, stronger relationships, heightened courage, and personal rewards that run deeper than spectacular jury verdicts.

It takes more than introspection to identify what we feel and why we feel that way. It also takes some bravery. Like many intelligent and educated people, attorneys tend to use intellectualizing as an emotional defense in their personal as well as professional lives. As the great science fiction writer Robert Heinlein once wrote, "Man is not a rational animal; he is a rationalizing animal." In other words, we may follow our gut, but we're not above second-guessing ourselves. It takes courage as well as work to overcome your natural psychological defenses and to feel uncomfortable. We all have these psychological defenses that serve to camouflage or control emotions that are painful and interfere with our ability to function well.

We learn how to cope with emotions by developing conscious and subconscious strategies to manage them. If we can't control a situation, these defenses override our emotions and help us get through the experience. Sometimes, our situations and emotions can overwhelm these defenses, and we experience problems functioning.

However, as you know now, emotions are an extraordinary advantage in life as well as in your profession, but only when they are understood and goal-directed. Increasing your emotional acuity will help you to become more credible and persuasive. Along the way, you might also discover aspects of yourself that are unrealized or unwanted, and as a result, you may change.

Chapter Two:

Voir Dire

I was working on a medical malpractice case when the jury pool was escorted into the courtroom to begin voir dire. One of the jurors was a middle-aged balding man wearing a three-piece suit and carrying a briefcase. He had a stern expression, almost a scowl, and the plaintiff's attorney and I simultaneously muttered, "Yipes," as the man filed in with twenty-five other potential jurors. He was obviously going to be a strong juror and likely an adverse juror. Successful businessmen are typically conservative and generally don't favor large plaintiff awards, no matter what the injury had been. The attorney and I both wanted to keep him off the jury.

After we'd used our last peremptory strike, the man was one of four potential jurors left. Then his number was called. Great. We could not dismiss him ourselves, so our only hope was that the man would admit he couldn't be fair so the judge would remove him for cause. That's what ultimately happened, but not for the reasons we expected.

The first word out of his mouth was that he could not be impartial in this case. When the judge asked him why, the man began to cry and explained in detail how his sister-in-law had been a victim of malpractice and had died as a result. When the man's brother had tried to find out what had happened, the doctor and the hospital lied and altered the woman's medical records to cover up their mistake. The death had torn his family apart, and the experience with the medical center had left the man bitter and suspicious about doctors, hospitals, and medical procedures in general. He would never trust them again. Although the judge dismissed the man from the jury, his voir dire comments were the best testimony we could have hoped for, and set the tone for the upcoming trial and were, in my opinion, a big reason why we won. The experience also helped teach me a lesson: Never make assumptions or fail to acknowledge your own biases when trying to ferret out the biases of others.

Had we proceeded to interview the businessman, very likely our assumption that he was "one of them" and would be opposed to our case might have been apparent to him. This would immediately put him on the defensive, prompting him to give measured responses rather than open and honest ones. This is the last thing you want going into voir dire.

Voir dire is crucial to your success at trial, not because you can remove biased people, but because it's your best opportunity to establish a good relationship with jurors. During voir dire, jurors are already collecting vital impressions and quietly deciding who they trust and which side they will support. It is your first chance to make a favorable impression on jurors.

Despite its importance, voir dire is one of the most neglected stages of trial preparation for most attorneys. They put it off until the last chaotic days before trial when they have no choice but to rush into the process and get through it as best they can.

Why Attorneys Fear Voir Dire

There are a number of reasons for that neglect. Many attorneys are simply anxious about meeting new people in a public forum or fear that they won't ask the right questions. They worry they'll appear nervous or flustered. They worry their questions will be met with bored silence. Deselecting jurors feels like guesswork to them, and they worry they'll keep the wrong jurors and dismiss the right ones. Attorneys appreciate precision and clear arguments, but voir dire feels fraught with uncertainty and chance. It requires attorneys to think fast, quickly pivot, and make instinctive decisions, and many attorneys aren't confident in their ability to do those things. And what if they get a judge who tries to run the process or keeps accusing them of improperly "arguing your case in voir dire"?

The best way to approach voir dire is with the same vulnerability and openness we talked about in the previous chapter. Understand that jurors are creating an impression of you and that those first impressions have a major impact on which side each juror ultimately takes. Voir dire is as much a social occasion as it is a legal proceeding. It's like that first dance in junior high school where everyone is checking everyone else out, nobody knows what to expect, and no one wants to make the first move. It's up to the plaintiff's attorney to show the courage to stride across the gym floor and invite someone to dance.

A successful outcome at trial depends on you persuading a group of citizens with diverse backgrounds and experiences that they should believe your version and interpretation of the evidence. The jury's understanding of that evidence and its significance depends on which attorney has established credibility and earned their trust. Voir dire is the first and best opportunity to establish that credibility and trust. Understanding the process of voir dire and how to properly prepare helps diminish much of this anxiety and will significantly increase the chances of a successful outcome at trial.

How to Prepare for Voir Dire

If you're preparing for voir dire, you need to take two crucial steps. The first is to examine your own biases about a case, and the second is to determine the meaning of your case.

1. Finding Your Own Blind Spots- Most attorneys think of voir dire as the process of identifying any juror biases that might hurt your case. But the most dangerous bias might be your own. If jurors have blind spots, so can you. Be open and honest with yourself: is there anything about your case or your client that might affect how you perform in this trial? We often aren't aware of our own biases, and it takes a lot of patience and soul-searching to discover them. It's worth the effort, however; your own biases will affect how you communicate with the jury, the type of questions you ask, or your demeanor while examining certain key witnesses, and if you aren't aware of that possibility, you could hurt your own case without knowing it.

An emotionally astute attorney will take the time to look at their own feelings and attitudes about the issues and personalities in their case. These issues are not technical matters regarding evidence and admissibility. Rather, they involve how you feel about the central issue in dispute or your feelings about the client or defendant. For example, if you dislike a difficult or eccentric client, it will certainly affect how you conduct your exam during the trial. If you have a harsh or discounting opinion of their experience of the damages, you need to question why you feel that way before you can effectively present that evidence to the jury. Jurors consider how you say what you say, how you discuss certain issues and evidence, and how you interact with witnesses.

The point here is that if you are *aware* of your bias, you are less likely to let it affect your case. Identifying and admitting your bias raises your self-awareness and confidence, and it can also help you gain the trust of the jury. Let me give you an example. In one case I worked on, the defendant was a large African-American man who stood six feet five inches and weighed over 300 pounds. He resembled the actor Michael Clarke Duncan in the 1999 film "The Green Mile,"huge and powerfully built. And like the character in the film, our client had been accused of a brutal murder.

The defendant had a history of violence. In fact, he was already in prison for murder when this latest incident occurred. The prison staff had discontinued his anti-psychotic medicine and transferred our client to a cell with a notorious pedophile. When the pedophile was found dead, our client was charged with the killing. When I asked the attorney what concerned him most about the case, he indicated he worried about how jurors would react to his client's imposing presence, mental health, and violent history.

"How could you *not* think this man was capable of violence?" the attorney told me. "I mean, *look at him.* He's huge, he's already convicted of murder, and he's mentally ill!" "Valid concerns," I replied. "Does the guy scare *you?*" The attorney looked out the window for a long moment. "He's always been polite and cooperative with me," the attorney said. "He's docile. He's like a child." "But … ?" "But, yeah, he scares the shit out of me," the attorney admitted. "When I'm alone with him in a room … this guy is a white person's worst nightmare." Now we were making progress to identifying the elephant in the room.

It turns out that the attorney had grown up in a racially divided city in a neighborhood torn apart by racial violence related to school integration and busing. He'd seen several violent encounters and had grown up with an everyday fear of Black people. As an adult, he tried to reject the racism of his childhood. But his perceptions were rooted in a visceral, persistent fear stemming from his childhood experiences, and he'd struggled to overcome this bias.

He was embarrassed to admit all this, but as we talked about his experiences and talked about the importance of being authentic with the jury, the discussion turned to how we could use his bias during voir dire to identify bias among jurors. As this idea emerged, he became less hesitant and began to use his own reactions to anticipate and plan for voir dire. A few days later in the courtroom at the beginning of voir dire, the attorney opened up to the pool of potential jurors:

I want to talk about some of the issues involved in this trial. Maybe after talking to each of you, we can decide together if this is the right case for you or not. The issue is not what you believe, or if you are a "fair person," but whether you can be fair in this case with these issues involved. I think that people are basically fair, or at least want to be fair. I believe you all want to be fair. Still, we all have experiences in life that cause us to have strong feelings or beliefs that make it difficult for us to be fair on a particular issue.

If you feel uncomfortable or hesitant discussing these feelings or beliefs, it's OK. Just let me know. I don't want to make you feel uncomfortable. I promise you that I will respect your honesty and integrity. I am in no position to judge you. I figured that if I expect you to be honest with me, I should start by being honest with you.

I grew up in Detroit in the early seventies. There was a lot of racial violence at that time, and I grew up feeling afraid of African-Americans. I like to think I've outgrown those fears, but to this day when I am walking down a street and see a group of Black men walking toward me, I get a different feeling than I do when it's a group of white men. When I see that group of Black men, I get nervous. I go on high alert. Because of the way I grew up, my brain sees that group of men as a threat, and I subconsciously get ready to fight or flee. It's automatic and reflexive, and I have to consciously work to overcome that reaction. It's getting better, but I still struggle with it.

So, those feelings affected me when I met my client for the first time. As you can see, he is a big guy. I knew he'd already been convicted of a violent crime, and I knew he had schizophrenia. My innate feelings caused me to assume something about him, even though I didn't know him and hadn't even spoken with him yet! Now, he's never given me a reason to be afraid of him. He's always been calm and cooperative. But I was still uncomfortable at times, and as I asked myself why that was, I realized that I had these deep seated emotions from childhood. Being able to label those emotions and see where they come from helps me to set them aside and view my client differently.

I'm embarrassed to tell you this. I'm not proud of how I feel sometimes, but I am proud that I've acknowledged my bias and am working to overcome it. I also figured that if I had to overcome these irrational feelings, some of you might be facing the same challenge. And that's what I want to talk about today. If you reacted the way I did, will you be able to set aside your irrational assumptions? How did you feel when you heard the charges of murder and saw my client this morning?

At first, the jury hesitated to say anything. Then they began to open up and share their own feelings and experiences. The attorney listened to each carefully, and as the jurors saw that the attorney stayed true to his word and respected their honesty and integrity, more began opening up.

Then, an African-American woman in the jury box dropped a bomb. "I'm not prejudiced and I'm sorry that you are," she said angrily. "How can you possibly represent this man when you feel the way you do?" Stunned silence filled the courtroom. I had a cold pit in my stomach and wanted to melt under the table. *This could get very bad*, I thought. My attorney nodded and made a resigned expression.

"I hear you," he said, nodding again. "That's a fair question. My first impulse when you asked it was to deny my prejudice and defend myself. But the truth is that you're right. I *am* still prejudiced. But I also think that because I am aware of that part of me, I am in a better position to help my client than someone who isn't aware of their bias or is too proud to admit it. I see it for what it is and I'm setting it aside. I'm here now because I hope that by discussing this issue we can all set it aside and give my client a fair jury and a fair trial." Something remarkable then happened. Other jurors- both white and black- began defending the attorney and talking about their own biases.

"Everybody has some prejudice ... I know I do," said one juror. "I grew up in Detroit, too, and I know what he's talking about," said another. "Most people are ready to move on from that," another insisted. As the comments flowed from prospective jurors, I could see that the attorney had become one of them. They were responding to his honesty and vulnerability. They identified with his personal struggle to become a better person, and they were eager to join him in that rewarding effort. It took tremendous courage for my attorney to respond to the African-American juror the way he did, but it gave him credibility and the jury's trust.

Racism is a common bias, but there are many others and it's always best to bring them to the surface during voir dire. Keep in mind that although some self-disclosure helps jurors understand the process and open up about their own biases, excessive self-disclosure can hurt your credibility. It must be true and related to the case. You don't want to give the idea that you're simply "fishing" for hidden biases. The occasional self-disclosure is a powerful way to develop a connection with the jury.

Introspection and being honest about your own biases will pay off later when you present your case. If you don't like your client for some reason, you need to figure out why and decide whether you can set that bias aside and present a strong case for them. The most dangerous unrecognized biases are your own, but if you take time to find and acknowledge those biases and discuss them openly and honestly, your voir dire will be far more effective.

2. Finding the Meaning of Your Case- One way to uncover the issues and biases that you want to address during voir dire is to develop the "meaning" of your case. Every case is a story. It has characters and it has a plot. It has conflict. But it also has significance and lessons, and this is where you'll discover the meaning of your case.

The meaning of a case is what you believe happened—the factual details—as well as *why* something happened and what impact it had on your client or others involved. Identifying the meaning of your case helps jurors perceive the evidence you present to them. In this sense, a driver who was T-boned in an intersection didn't just endure a crippling back injury. The driver was crippled at a time when he was starting a family or embarking on a new career or finally getting to enjoy life in retirement after a long career raising three children as a single dad. The meaning, then, is not just the crippling injury. It's the injustice. It's the permanent alteration of a person's hopes and dreams.

This was the context in which the collision occurred. It's a lot more than just another T-bone at a busy intersection. Damages are understood in the context of the client's life, and you must translate that significance to the jury. Attorneys often fail to appreciate the meaning of the damages to the client because of their own bias, and that bias will be communicated to the jurors during voir dire. Biases can emerge from the meaning attached by jurors to events, so you'll want to use voir dire to ferret that out. For instance, a prospective juror who asserts that retirement is a time when people should enjoy permanent bed rest would not help your case at trial.

Understanding the meaning of your case allows you to identify the issues that will affect your case and help you address them. To do that, you must know *why* those issues are important. Understanding why the issues are important will help you construct real questions based on that understanding.

For example, I did a case once where we represented a man who was crossing the street in a crosswalk when he was struck and badly injured by a driver going through the intersection. The only issue was that our client had a blood-alcohol level of .20 at the time. He was legally drunk. This might lead some jurors to think the guy was a less-worthy victim. But there is no law against walking around drunk and there is no law about using a crosswalk while drunk. Our client's drunkenness didn't contribute to the accident in any way. In that case, Ven had to be open and honest and try to get the jury to open up about a polarizing issue- using alcohol. So, he asked the jury point-blank: Does anyone think less of my client because he was drunk at the time he was hit?

Once you know the story you must tell, you will know what the issues are in your case and have a sense of the issues you need to explore during voir dire. One goal of voir dire is to identify the most pertinent biases and those jurors who hold those biases closely. And, as we've already discussed, this process begins by doing your own self voir dire focusing on what your biases and obstacles may be. By considering your own biases and concerns about what you perceive are the issues in the case, you will identify some of the issues that you might have otherwise overlooked. As I said, we all have our blind spots and becoming aware of those issues will help reveal biases similar to what the prospective jurors will have.

Three Types of Biases

Understanding your own bias is the most challenging issue, but not the only one. Spotting the biases in jurors is equally challenging, and it's crucial that you react properly to those biases.

The most common biases come from three different types of jurors- ideological jurors, stealth jurors, and jurors with unrecognized biases.

1. Ideological Jurors- Ideological jurors have a personal and political agenda, and they see jury trials as a vehicle to validate their beliefs. These beliefs can take many forms. Minorities are criminal and violent. Lawsuits are undermining law and order. Plaintiffs are frauds and parasites. Corporations are evil. No amount of evidence or logic will change their mind. They come to the trial with an emotional need that resists facts or reality. No doubt you've met people like this. You might be related to someone like this.

They're a little easier to spot because they typically can't wait to tell you what's wrong with you and your case. The only meaning they derive from your story is from the random facts that support their beliefs. How do you deal with them? It takes more than a little patience and emotional acuity. You can't argue with them or react defensively because you risk isolating yourself from the other jurors. As attorney Gerry Spence once put it, the jury is a tribe, and if you go after one of them, the others may rally to their defense, even if they disagree with the juror's ideology. It's the same dynamic you see in families; if someone attacks a family member, we come to their defense, even when we know they were wrong or behaving like a jerk.

Some attorneys worry that ideological jurors, with their unrelenting and warped perspective, will "poison the well" and turn the rest of the jury against you. If you don't react defensively, that won't happen. Respectfully listen to their views, but don't engage in a debate or quickly dismiss their answers. Accept what they say with the same courtesy you give all the jurors. If you appear reasonable, the ideologue will eventually isolate themselves from the rest of the jury with their unbalanced harangues.

2. The Stealth Juror- Stealth jurors have the same ardent beliefs as the ideologue but they hide them in hopes of getting on a jury and undermining the case. Stealth jurors give answers that tend to be too perfect for plaintiff cases. They sound like they would support your side, but there is something just too pat about their answers. They sound like they're reading off a script, and they lack spontaneity and humor. You might think initially that the person is just nervous, but the lack of emotion and sincerity soon becomes the prevailing quality of their responses. You develop a gut sense that they are malignantly hiding something.

Use your emotional insights as an early warning system. If you find yourself uncomfortable for some reason with a juror who seems to have responded with favorable answers to your questions, then evaluate that sense. Why do you feel that way? What aspect of the juror's response prompted the concern, or what aspect of yourself is responding to them? Ultimately you have to be comfortable with that juror or you may find yourself second-guessing or being overly attentive or sensitive to that juror's reactions during the trial.

Take the time to evaluate your gut feeling and understand it. There are times when the idiosyncrasies of a juror may mislead you, but by asking more focused questions, you can spot that stealth juror and reveal their bias. Sometimes, stealth jurors don't bother to hide their bias and instead insist that they can set their bias aside. This prevents them from being dismissed by the judge and it forces you to use a peremptory challenge.

I worked on one case involving a trucker who was killed in a loading dock accident. One of the prospective jurors was a woman who worked as a secretary in her husband's insurance adjuster's business. Her business depended on *avoiding* lawsuits. She admitted to believing that most personal injury lawsuits are frivolous and that they add to the cost of insurance for everyone. "But I can be fair," she insisted. In fact, she mentioned that over and over again. Those are the magic words for a judge; as long as a juror assures the judge they will remain fair, the judge will never dismiss them for cause. As we questioned her, she said one thing after another to indicate that she would not support the plaintiff's case, but she always concluded by saying, "But I can be fair." This was deliberate sabotage, in my opinion.

The mistake my attorney made was to keep probing. He wanted the judge to dismiss her so he could keep his last peremptory challenge, but this woman was too good. After about five questions, I started handing my attorney notes saying, "Let her go," and "She's not going to admit to a bias," and so on.

But he kept after her. He was determined to get enough evidence to make a strike-for-cause motion. His questions became more pointed and he became visibly frustrated. It was brutal. Finally, one of the defense attorneys objected, saying, "Judge, this has to stop. He's just badgering this poor woman!" In doing so, the defense attorney jumped to the defense of the juror but also to the aid of the other jurors, who were clearly relieved that the awkward confrontation was over. The judge ordered an end to the questioning and my attorney had to use his final peremptory challenge to remove the woman. She was replaced by a young male juror, who introduced himself and then addressed my attorney. "And yes," he said flatly, "You were badgering that woman." My attorney had lost credibility and trust and, ultimately, he lost the trial.

3. Unrecognized Bias- The third and most common type of bias comes from jurors who want to be fair but are unaware of their own prejudice. The trick for a plaintiff's attorney is to help these jurors recognize their bias without offending them or galvanizing the rest of the jury around them. When a bias the juror was unaware of is revealed, you must explicitly ally yourself with their desire to be fair rather than try and change their belief. "Mr. Jones, I'm not sure I fully understand what you mean," you might say. "Can you further explain why you feel that way?"

Being authentic and honest about your own biases goes a long way toward helping jurors see and admit their hidden biases. If you articulate the bias as one you hold, they are more likely to identify it in themselves and be comfortable discussing it with you.

Attorney Steve Fishman did this brilliantly during a voir dire in a criminal trial. Here's how he addressed the jury pool during voir dire:

Does everyone here believe in the right to be presumed innocent until proven guilty? Of course! We all value that belief, especially me. As an attorney who represents people accused of crimes, you better believe I think that right is important.

But believing in the right to be presumed innocent is sometimes different from how we really think and act.

For example, when I'm driving down the freeway and I see a state trooper putting handcuffs on a man pulled over, I don't think to myself, "Gee, I wonder what that guy is presumed innocent of doing!" No. I wonder what that guy did wrong to get arrested. He must have done something wrong or the cop wouldn't be handcuffing him. The presumption of innocence exists as a principle we want to hold, but something else guides our perceptions when someone else is being arrested by the police.

In this instance, Steve threw in with the jury. He was one of them. He, too, wrestled with hypocrisy, just like they did. We're all wrestling with this bias! We need to remember that the guy in handcuffs isn't guilty. He's innocent until someone proves he did something wrong. Because he shared the same bias as the jurors, his voir dire questions seemed less threatening. Jurors felt safe in admitting, like Steve had, that they could be prejudiced, too.

How to Ask Questions

The purpose of voir dire is not to argue your case or test reactions to evidence. The most crucial goal is to establish a good relationship with jurors. If they trust you, they will speak openly and honestly about their biases during voir dire and give greater credence to you later when you present evidence. Voir dire is your only opportunity for a meaningful conversation with jurors. Remember, it's a social process. You are a complete stranger to jurors, so coming across as authentic and interested goes a long way to reassuring jurors and convincing them that it's safe to disclose sensitive, personal information. How you ask questions and listen to the answers is a vital part of that process.

Follow the same rules during voir dire that you would in any other important social setting. Show authentic interest in what jurors do and say. Be forthright, curious, and inviting. This is the most challenging aspect of voir dire skills because it requires you to do the hard work of understanding how you feel about your case and why. It requires that you find the courage to be frank and upfront with jurors. This does not mean that you *project* an image of authenticity- jurors can tell when you are being artificial - but that you are genuinely sincere. Sometimes an attorney will try too hard to project sincerity, and it is perceived as contrived or phony. There is no substitute for authenticity. If you are asking yourself, "How can I show jurors how much I care about..." then you are not being authentic. You must understand your own emotions and work your voir dire with those in mind.

When preparing for voir dire, outline the questions and key issues you want to discuss but also the order in which issues are introduced. Remember, it's a conversation. It's not a cross-examination. There should be a flow to the discussion, and some issues should be discussed before others. One example is compensation; you should never introduce the idea of compensation until you've probed areas regarding liability and injuries. It's only after the context of your case is explained that jurors are mentally prepared to talk about damages. Prepare, but don't be a slave to your outline; follow the flow when the conversation pivots to another issue. Here are some other key points to remember about voir dire:

1. Ask Honest Questions- Avoid insincere or dishonest questions, such as "Do you think people should be held accountable for their mistakes?" or "Do you think the police should be allowed to shoot innocent people?" These questions are not intended to get information but to make a point or argue the case. Attorneys who ask questions with obvious answers are perceived as phony or untrustworthy. If everyone would answer the question the same way, then it's not a real question and you'll lose credibility by asking it. Here are some dishonest questions you want to be sure to avoid:

- "Ma'am, what is your style of parenting? Do you teach your children to do the right thing?"
- "Is there anybody here who would not base their verdict on the evidence or follow the law?"
- "Is there anybody here who thinks that it's OK for a doctor to harm a patient?"
- "Is there anyone here who believes it is acceptable to discriminate against people in the workplace?"
- "Is it important to obey traffic laws at all times?"

You get the idea. I've heard all of these questions asked during voir dire, sometimes by new attorneys and sometimes by veteran attorneys. Both should know better.

2. Try to Connect with Each Juror- How many times have you heard an attorney ask a juror what job they work, or do they have a family, and then, without any meaningful response or after a perfunctory "thank you," quickly move on to

ask another juror the same questions? How does that juror feel? How will the next juror respond? Dismissed? Unimportant? Do not neglect a juror during voir dire.

Remain unfailingly open, honest, and attentive with jurors. Some jurors are expecting you to be shifty, so give them a reason to trust you and believe what you say. This is easier for some lawyers than for others, but it's a big challenge for anyone. It requires practice. A little honest self-disclosure and a sincere interest in what others think help put jurors at ease.

3. Be Curious- Don't miss opportunities to ask about some interesting aspects of a juror's life if they bring them up. People enjoy it when someone has a genuine interest in their life. It helps them to feel comfortable talking about other aspects of their lives. Knowing what you want to accomplish in voir dire will help you stay on track while still exploring any little side trails that appear.

Follow the juror's lead. Sometimes jurors will introduce an unrelated topic. When they do, probe it a bit. Sometimes this is the juror's approach to "feeling their way" to the central issue, so listen carefully and respond. If nothing else, it shows you care, and if the topic is too far afield, you can quickly bring it back to the issue you really want to discuss.

4. Start Slowly- Start with the less challenging issues and work toward the most difficult issues after you have established an atmosphere of comfort and safety. The sequence of voir dire questions should have a natural flow, with one issue leading to the next and voir dire on one issue helping to set up the next.

Consider the approach used by Von Johnson. He starts out talking with potential jurors about their lives, occupations, and interests before he begins gently probing them about their biases against lawsuits and damages. "Most people feel there are too many lawsuits and too many large verdicts rendered," Ven says. "But when I probe their 'personal knowledge' about these issues, most people admit they've never filed a lawsuit or know anyone who ever received a large, unwarranted jury verdict."

5. Be Human- Listen to what a juror is saying and respond as you would in a conversation. Sometimes that might mean taking a moment to feel your reaction to their answer and understand it. You might then tell the juror how their answer made you feel and why, leading to a more honest and open discussion.

For instance, if it's a wrongful death case and the juror mentions how their father died in a tragic accident, it's okay to react on a personal level. "I am so sorry to hear about the circumstance of your dad's death," you might say. "My dad died too and it was horrible for me. I know it affected some of the ways I think about the issues in this case. How do you think your dad's death could come into play if you sat on the jury?" Some attorneys feel this type of response is unprofessional or somehow violates protocol, but jurors are rarely offended and are often impressed with the spontaneity and humanity of the attorney. This is just being a normal human being responding to another, which can only increase trust and credibility.

6. Avoid Legalese- Lawyers use legal jargon all the time with fellow attorneys, judges, clerks, and even police officers. But using legal terms or phrases during voir dire is only going to confuse jurors and leave them suspicious. Throwing around a lot of jargon can also intimidate them and make them less likely to be open with their responses. If you need to explain a legal term, use plain language that laypeople can understand.

7. Remember, It's a Conversation- When a juror shares personal information, they deserve an acknowledgment from you, whether it is a follow-up question, a comment, or a simple, sincere "thank you." We've all seen attorneys with questions on a legal pad; they ask a question, make a checkmark on their pad, and move on to the next question or juror. If you are at a dinner party and a guest asks you about your life, fails to respond, and then goes on to ask the same question to another person, how does it make you feel? Dismissed or unimportant? How does it make you feel about the person asking the question? On the other hand, when someone you are just meeting expresses a genuine interest in some aspect of your life or your opinion, it encourages conversation. Find a common point of interest with a juror and engage them. This will encourage identification with you, and people tend to trust others who are similar.

Dealing with 'Adverse' Jurors

When a juror has an adverse response or is just plain rude and combative, you can't engage with them in a reactive manner. . You can't get defensive. You can't attempt to outdebate them. You can't show frustration with them. You can say you feel disappointed with the opinion while still communicating respect and approval for their response and for being honorable enough to be honest.

Being patient and kind to an adverse juror will earn your trust with jurors. Confronting a juror, even after it may seem obvious to everyone that they are biased, could alienate jurors. I have seen several attorneys lose trials by overzealously trying to construct a basis "for cause" the way the attorney in the trucking accident did in the trial we discussed earlier in this chapter. It does not benefit you to strike one juror if it alienates the remaining jury pool. When trying to expose bias in a juror, use the Golden Rule; treat them as you want to be treated. Don't assume other jurors see the same bias you see.

Some attorneys try to shut down a biased juror, thinking that they'll poison the jury pool, but the other jurors will see what you're doing and think less of you for it. They'll think you're trying to squelch opposing viewpoints. Responding to an adverse answer with curiosity and equanimity, on the other hand, shows you're confident in your case.

Remaining silent in the face of an adverse response is a missed opportunity to build trust with the rest of the jury pool. Your response has to be honest but it can't sound defensive. Focus instead on reinforcing the fact that the juror was honest and that you respect and appreciate that honesty.

For example, you might say, "I understand what you're saying, and I do respect it. I may not agree with it, but that is your opinion, and I really respect you for how you are being honest about it. So, let me ask you this, if you were picking the jury on behalf of my client, do you understand why your belief would make it hard for me to believe you'll be fair in this particular trial?"

You can also use the direct approach: "Does your belief make it too hard for you to be fair in this trial? I wonder if it would be unfair to put you in a position where you had to ignore your beliefs and sit on the jury in this trial. How would you be able to ignore such a strong belief and honestly consider the other side?"

Defending a Juror

In the example above, the attorney is defending the honesty of the juror and not their bias. That is an important distinction that will matter a lot to the other jurors who may, or may not, agree with them. I was involved in one case where we were able to defend a juror and gain some measure of support from the jury as a whole. The case involved an injury to a newborn baby in a hospital, and one of the jurors we interviewed came across as protective and nurturing but also shy. I had correctly sensed that she had experienced trauma herself as a child and encouraged the attorney to defend her from any defense challenge. The plaintiff's attorney and I agreed that we would ask her very few questions and not give the defense much to work with. If the defense challenged her for cause, then we would oppose the motion vigorously.

During the defendant's voir dire, the defense attorney asked the woman if she could be fair to both sides. She paused for a moment, but then answered, "Yes, I think I can." The defense asked that she be removed. They argued that she was not honest because she had hesitated to answer the question about fairness. My attorney sprang to his feet. "Judge, just because this woman took the time to consider his question and respond thoughtfully doesn't give him the right to attack her and accuse her of dishonesty," he said. "It's obvious she was being sincere and honest."

It was as though he used a Jedi mind technique. When the judge responded, he mirrored the plaintiff's attorney. "Just because this juror took the time to consider your question does not suggest to me that she was being dishonest," the judge said. "Motion denied." It was a foolish and unfair attack by the defense attorney, and it alienated many of the jurors.

We went on to win the case for a staggering amount of money. After the trial, we learned that the jurors felt the defense attorney was "dishonest." The meek, mild-mannered woman we defended became our champion and was instrumental in the deliberations on the life care plan evidence, paving the way for the $128 million verdict. Here are some additional tips for dealing with adverse jurors:

1. Don't Get Defensive- Instead of responding to an answer defensively, respond with questions that encourage an adverse juror to explain their answer or the reasons why they feel the way they do. Asking them to help you understand what they are thinking encourages more dialogue and could help you construct a strike argument. In many instances, it leads to the juror admitting that they couldn't be fair at trial.

Sometimes adverse jurors will get on a "soapbox" and go on and on. Even in that situation try to be accepting of their opinion (or bias). Jurors with a similar bias are encouraged to volunteer their biases (saving you the time) or others in the venire will come to recognize the bias of those jurors (making it more conducive for striking them without appearing to attack other jurors). Again, confronting a juror, even confronting a juror who is obviously not being truthful, can alienate a jury. Accepting and trying to understand a juror's bias will help you establish trust with the entire jury. This advice is certainly easier said than done It takes awareness and honesty to recognize when we become defensive. In fact, it takes hard work in and out of the courtroom, but the rewards of this work on yourself will be worth it.

2. Show Respect- In some instances when a juror goes on with an obvious bias, it can stimulate another juror to voice an opposing opinion. This is a real

blessing for the attorney because a conversation among jurors is optimal to identify not only their opinions as individuals but also how they work with other jurors. When this happens, stay out of the way and learn.

A juror who expresses a hostile opinion is doing you a favor. You can express respect for the person without condoning their bias. If you remain open and accepting of their response, striking the juror will be seen by other jurors as logical and reasonable. It will enhance your credibility. Responding defensively, on the other hand, leads to confrontational questions. This will not only shut down the juror but the entire venire. Worst yet, you run the risk of alienating other jurors who identify with their fellow jurors. They could perceive your reaction as an attack on one of their brothers.

3. Let Them Deselect Themselves- Even when a juror admits they can't be fair, never assume you have sufficient evidence for a challenge. You have to preempt any attempt by the judge to rehabilitate them. To do that, follow up any bias admission by reaffirming with the juror their assertion that they can't be fair. Firmly plant the admission in the courtroom's mind. Then caution the juror that the judge is soon going to ask the juror if he can be fair. Remind the juror that it's difficult to say "no" to a judge. Then, using the same language the judge is likely to use, solidify their admission.

"In a moment or two, the judge is going to tell you that you must set aside your beliefs and consider only the evidence," you might say. "It's awfully hard to tell a judge that even if you tried, you don't think you can be fair. But what I hear you saying to me is that no matter who asks you, you can't be sure you could set your beliefs aside even if you tried. Is that fair to say?"

Now, it's no guarantee that the juror, under pressure from the judge, won't suddenly find it in himself to declare himself unbiased and fair. But it will be clear that a change in response is only because of who is asking and not because they suddenly became impartial.

***

Forming a Bond with Jurors

When we meet someone who seems to be asking questions to make a point or to try and direct us to a certain point of view, we become suspicious. On the other hand, when we meet someone who shows genuine interest in our point of view and is clearly absorbing our answers and responding with related questions, we're more engaged ourselves. We feel a bond forming.

Ven Johnson is a master at developing this instant, open rapport with jurors. Skilled attorneys truly listen to each juror's response to the questions, even if the answer is probably negative toward the attorney or their case.

I've watched Ven work on several cases. His manner is natural and friendly. He encourages jurors to expand on their statements and asks pointed follow-up questions that show that he is closely listening and cares. Sometimes all he does is repeat three or four keywords from what the person said. This "mirroring" technique opens the door to more expansive and telling comments from the juror. When he hears an opinion that he doesn't agree with—and everyone in the room *knows* he doesn't agree with—he never loses his concerned, genuine demeanor. "I respect your opinion," he'll say. "Please help me understand more about how or why you feel so strongly." When a juror reveals a personal tragedy, Ven sympathizes, labeling the tragedy as something that would certainly have a big impact on the person's worldview.

It's an unfortunate irony that unbiased jurors are more likely to equivocate about their ability to be fair while biased jurors are adamant about their ability to remain open-minded. The best approach for any attorney when a juror equivocates is to respond with curiosity rather than suspicion. The truly fair juror is just being honest; they can't be absolutely sure they will be fair because they don't know. All they know is that they have the capacity to reflect and consider other perspectives. The juror who guarantees fairness usually lacks the capacity for introspection and insight.

If you ask the right questions in the right way, you can get a juror to recognize and talk about an unrecognized bias in a way that educates and edifies rather than embarrasses or offends. Prod gently, accept answers without qualification, and convey your respect to every juror. The juror who can say in effect, "Now that you mention it, I guess I do have an issue about this" is a juror who may be able to overcome that bias or will deselect themselves. The juror who can self-identify the bias with your help may not be deselected in the end but will be aware of their bias during trial. So will their fellow jurors during deliberations.

***

Conclusion and Key Takeaways

I've debriefed juries after trials dozens of times, and whenever jurors are asked about what made an attorney credible or trustworthy after voir dire, the responses are consistent:

- The attorney asked "real" questions. These are questions that genuinely seek information from jurors, as distinct from questions with obvious answers, or questions that try to make a point.
- The attorney was listening and responding to what the jurors were saying. The attorney seemed to have an interest in their answers, and a curiosity about them.
- The attorney was "talking" with them, rather than just asking questions. The attorney seemed spontaneous and not "fake" or "contrived." The attorney wasn't talking at them or interrogating them.
- The attorney seemed easy to talk with, just like a regular person. The attorney seemed comfortable and helped them to feel comfortable.
- The attorney admitted he was nervous, which made him seem more human to jurors. "We were nervous too, but his comment put us at ease and made us want to help him," said one juror I interviewed.
- The attorney didn't "judge" the jurors' answers. The attorney tried to understand the answer rather than debate it or dismiss it.

Note that most favorable comments relate to *how* the attorney conducted the voir dire rather than the substance of the questions themselves. Once again, this shows that voir dire is not a McCarthy hearing to ferret out opposition sympathizers. It's a social gathering. It's a meet-and-greet. It's a way for attorneys to get to know who they will be working with, and *that's* information that will pay off throughout the trial.

Chapter Three:
Voir Dire on Damages

Some politicians, defense lawyers, and doctors would have you believe that we need tort reform because juries are irresponsible and happily award outrageous sums for a plaintiff's pain and suffering. In fact, the opposite is true. In malpractice cases, doctors win the overwhelming majority. And in all personal injury cases, malpractice and otherwise, most juries have a bias against monetary awards for noneconomic losses like pain and suffering. They are typically skeptical of large damage awards, and, according to one recent study, the uncertainty about how to measure pain and suffering leads to lower awards.

Noneconomic damages include mental anguish, loss of companionship, reduced quality of life, disability, disfigurement, loss of vision or hearing, and loss of enjoyment in life. The problem for juries is clear. *How do you measure the value of any one of those things?* It's a confounding question, and our court system doesn't provide a template to help jurors figure it out. While compensation for economic damages requires an accounting of the actual damages, compensation for "bodily harm" and "emotional distress" can be awarded "without proof of pecuniary loss." Juries are merely told to be "reasonable."

The uncertainty leads some jurors to struggle greatly. *What's reasonable? What's fair? How do you measure something like "anguish" or "loss of companionship?"* Some jurors believe that if you can't calculate the loss, you can't compensate someone for it. Other jurors can't put a monetary value on something that you would never take money to suffer. Still others have listened to the tort reform propaganda and believe lawsuits are bad for society and that noneconomic damages are the reason. For these reasons, voir dire on damages can feel nothing short of treacherous.

Uncomfortable Elements

No one likes to talk about pain, suffering, and disability. These and other noneconomic damages are wrapped up in the human experience. We all experience betrayal by a friend, a broken promise, a moment of withering public derision. That's life. Sometimes these misfortunes are brought about by wrongdoing, but often, they *just happen* and we're rarely compensated for that kind of suffering. However, our legal system requires fair compensation for these injuries, and that concept flies in the face of what we perceive to be the nature of the human experience. We all experience profound loss, but most of us never get paid for our trouble.

Another uncomfortable element is the idea of money itself. The plaintiff lost a child in a medical accident or they were injured badly by another driver. Of course, they should be compensated for the income they lost, the vehicle they have to replace, and their medical bills. But how do they determine a price tag for the plaintiff's emotional trauma over losing a child?

This is what you're up against when you voir dire on damages. You must voir dire on damages in every trial, however, and to succeed, you must focus on the idea of *compensation as a means of doing justice*. You have to help the jury realize that, in a courtroom, justice is measured by compensation.

Compensation is the only mechanism available. It may feel crass to some people, and it may feel random and uncertain to those who prefer to follow a formula and make a precise calculation. However, you must convince the jury to set aside their confusion and reservations. It is the jury's duty to decide on justice, and when it comes to pain and suffering, the only form of justice is money.

According to a recent study at Cornell University, three factors affect pain-and-suffering awards:

1. How much the plaintiff suffered and how much their injuries interfered with their lives- Ironically, how much the plaintiff suffered did not have as much impact on the award as the second calculation; the more jurors talked about how an individual's life was disrupted, the more they awarded.

2. Compensation anchors- Although I strongly advise against discussing precise compensation amounts during voir dire (I'll discuss why in a moment),

eventually a compensation anchor can lead to significantly higher compensation awards.

3. Liability- Although jurors are often instructed to focus on determining damages, they often "fuse" the liability and damage questions. Jurors who believe the defendant didn't act intentionally or with malice tend to give lower noneconomic damage awards.

How We View Pain and Suffering

The first step in preparing your voir dire on money damages is to examine your own biases about the damages in your case. Our own emotional defenses also play a role in understanding, valuing, and presenting the injuries clients suffer. This is especially true with the issue of pain and suffering.

We're all raised to view pain and suffering in different ways. Our gender, culture, and personal experiences all shape how we view it and place value on it. For example, I was raised by a single mom, and my two siblings and I lived on the edge of poverty. My mother suffered from depression, but she never let on to us about her pain and suffering. She didn't want her children to see her worried and afraid. Rather, she chose to devote heroic efforts to providing for us and protecting us from feelings of hopelessness.

As an adult, I came to realize that I was the same way with my own children. So were my siblings with their families. In hard times, we isolated ourselves, put our heads down, and worked to provide for our families. We took responsibility.

The point here is that experiences and beliefs we acquire through life can prevent us from understanding how a client in a courtroom is experiencing pain and suffering. If you're an attorney, you have to understand how your own experiences and beliefs make you feel about your client. You also have to acknowledge how experiences and beliefs will affect how jurors feel. Is it their belief that people have to bear their misfortune with silent courage? If so, how do you bring them around to understanding that their job in the courtroom is to mete out justice and that to do that, they may have to set aside those preconceptions?

Believe it or not, most attorneys underestimate the monetary value of damages. I know that sounds counter to the stereotype of the greedy lawyer, but the truth is that these attorneys often fail to understand the type and meaning of damages to the client. How we experience an injury might be vastly different from how the client experiences it. Everyone's sense of self and their place in the world is different. A disfigurement may not seem as devastating to some as it does to others. The loss of an ability to work in their chosen field might be a temporary setback for some but a life-altering tragedy for someone else. The depth of pain and suffering is not the same for everyone. Jurors will be asked to understand this, and they never will if the attorney doesn't.

I also frequently hear attorneys apologize to juries for the amount of money they are seeking for their clients. This is a big mistake. It sends the message that they are not convinced they're asking for the right amount. When I hear an attorney say, "I know it's a lot of money, but …" or "If you think that's too much, then …" I can see that they are bidding against themselves, discounting their case. If an attorney ever thinks a certain money value will "alienate" a jury, it's a sign that they lack commitment or have an emotional block preventing them from fully appreciating the pain and suffering their client has endured. These attorneys would be wise to identify their own experiences and beliefs and set them aside so they can focus on understanding their client's pain and suffering.

How Jurors View Damages

You must ask potential jurors about how they feel about compensation for pain and suffering, but it's a mistake to discuss a specific amount during voir dire unless you lay some groundwork first. During voir dire, jurors have no context for your case. You have not described the meaning of the case to them yet. The only context jurors have is a likely bias against plaintiffs seeking excessive money amounts.

What's more, as we've already mentioned, most jurors find it demeaning to put a monetary value on damages to compensate for the invaluable or irreplaceable. What's more, their frame of reference on compensation amounts is not the injury to the plaintiff but their own relationship with money. Let me explain.

When jurors hear during voir dire that they will be asked to "award" an amount of money that is many times what they will ever see in their lives, they often react with skepticism or cynicism. They have not heard the evidence or heard you describe the meaning of the case yet, so the only way they can interpret the amount you throw out is through their own personal financial circumstances.

Say, for instance, they're told they will be asked to compensate the plaintiff $20 million for a spine injury caused by the defendant. They think, *Twenty million dollars? How can any injury be worth that much?* It is an astronomical amount for most people, and that almost incomprehensible amount will sit in the jurors' minds and become the filter through which everything they hear must pass. This is always a disadvantage for the plaintiff. The jurors' natural response is to evaluate each individual piece of evidence by questioning whether it is worth twenty million dollarys.

Instead of considering *all* of the evidence on damages as a whole and how it affects the client, *then* placing a monetary value on all of the damages, they are forced to value the evidence piecemeal. For example, saying an elderly client is unable to play golf anymore due to pain and disability is valid evidence of damages. However, most jurors don't play golf and if they ask the question, "Is not being able to play golf worth a hundred million dollars?" the answer is, "No." There may be other evidence of damages, but with each succeeding answer of no, the value of *all* the evidence is diminished. The specific amount of damages becomes an impossible criterion to meet before all of the evidence is presented, understood, and *felt* by jurors.

Again, this is not to say you shouldn't voir dire on money damages. You must. But before discussing the range of damages being considered, you must identify and discuss the prevailing bias against compensation money for pain and suffering.

One Approach to Use

I worked with one attorney who navigated these tricky waters beautifully. Here's what he told the jury during voir dire:

Money as compensation is the only way justice can be done in a civil trial like this. There is no eye for an eye; we are not asking you to punish the defendant in any way. Justice is not about them and what they did. Rather, your job as a jury is to do right by their victim and repair the damage done as best we can. When it's not possible to repair, our job is to compensate them for the injury as they experienced it. We're not setting a price for their suffering or death; we are setting the price for justice.

If you decide that the defendant harmed my client, you will have to do something very difficult: put a money value as compensation for that damage. This is difficult because none of us outside of a courtroom would ever consider putting a price tag on damages in this way. But we are not outside the courtroom. We are in a trial, and money is the only way a jury can do justice.

I have a real dilemma in every case like this when asking for money as compensation. I'm required to ask for a specific amount of money as compensation. I always worry that if I ask for too much money, the jury will get mad at me and not give me any money as the result. On the other hand, if I don't ask for enough money, then I am cheating my client. But I am required to suggest a specific amount. All I can do is suggest an amount that I think is fair and let the evidence speak for itself.

I don't know if you anticipate that I will ask for as much money as I can get or as much money as I think is fair compensation. I can only promise you that I will not ask for a penny more than what I truly believe is fair.

So, the question I have to ask is this: if you think the amount that I suggest is too much, how would you react? Would you think I was being a money-grabber and react by lowering the amount you might compensate? Or would you be able to think "well that's what he thinks is fair, let me think about the evidence again?"

Once he acknowledged the challenges and labeled the dilemma facing jurors in cases like this, the attorney went on to gently probe the bias. "If I didn't prove my case, would any of you have a problem not providing any money as compensation?" Jurors almost always respond, "No," without hesitation. "Good. That's fair if I don't prove my case, and it's the way it's supposed to work. But, what if I asked it this way: if I do prove the case, would you have any problems compensating a lot of money, say $500 million?" The response is usually hesitant and often negative.

Now it feels a little different, doesn't it? I have to tell you that most of the time I ask that question, I see the same response, and this is a worry in every case. Why do you think it is that we have no problem deciding on no money if the evidence doesn't prove damages, but we all hesitate to provide the money even if the evidence does prove it? What do you think it is that makes us hesitant to accept money as compensation to a person even if justified by the evidence?

Voir dire is an opportunity to probe biases toward money as compensation without triggering jurors' skepticism or cynicism. This discussion about bias on money compensation also goes a long way toward identifying jurors for deselection. It's best to address these issues head-on. Acknowledge the challenge facing jurors but frame their responsibilities as jurors. Here's how the attorney I worked with did that:

"Some damages I can prove in a precise amount, like lost income or medical costs. But some damages are not easy to replace because there is no amount of money that can undo the damage done. They are also things that we never think about in terms of money value. For example, how do you feel about money as compensation for pain and suffering caused by another person?"

During voir dire, this attorney gave jurors time and space to form their answers. He was asking them to consider a question few people are ever confronted with, so he was sure to give them time to ponder the tough question. Then he moved on to probe a little deeper.

We all have experienced pain and suffering in our lives, but probably no one has ever offered us money. But what if someone else, through no fault of their own, is forced to experience pain and suffering by another person? What if someone inflicts that pain on them? What if medicine can't repair or replace the damage done to a person who was injured? What is the fair and just approach to that?

His delivery was key. He ran the risk of making some jurors think he was trying to lead them to the answer he wanted, something that would cause him to lose trust, but he avoided sounding rhetorical. Instead, he sounded like it was a question he, himself, had been forced to consider. Then he went on and framed the jury's responsibility:

We all experience pain and suffering, but we don't think about how much it is worth or getting money as compensation. Some things we would never think about putting a monetary value on, such as our ability to live independently, or to live without constant pain. But that is your job as jurors. Can you do that? Can you put a monetary value on something that you have never thought about in terms of money as compensation?

Finally, having labeled their dilemma, outlined their responsibility, and posed the overarching philosophical question, he zeroed in on the questions at hand. Do you think a person should be given money as compensation for pain and suffering inflicted? Do you think the person who caused the pain and suffering should offer money as compensation?

Focusing on money compensation as conflicting with some fundamental values we all hold (e.g. our health), helps to prepare for a more focused discussion during voir dire on the conflict we all have between our values and our willingness to compensate. It also primes the arguments to be used during closing. During closing, you can expand and compel the argument on monetary compensation and have the benefit of all the evidence on how the damages have affected the client.

"I don't know how to put a money value on…" or "What good is money if it won't stop the pain or heal the disability?" are normal responses. When you hear them, return to the discussion of money as the only means of justice allowed. The real question is, *What is the cost to justice if we don't compensate for suffering caused by injustice?* What is a gentle confrontation on this bias during voir dire becomes a central argument later during closing. Why do we think of money compensation for noneconomic damages as somehow enriching a victim for something money could never buy? The reality is that monetary compensation is more of a kind of consolation as it is an award.

Voir Dire on Comparative Negligence

Another factor to keep in mind during voir dire on damages is the common human belief that we have control over what happens to us. Having a sense of control is a primary task of the brain (or mind) as it has evolved. Therefore, it is an essential element of persuasion. We all resist the idea that we can't control the world or prevent devastating injuries to ourselves or our loved ones. This bias surfaces in all personal injury cases, but it's especially prevalent in cases where comparative negligence is alleged. It's the reason why, absent any explanation, people explain an event as "an act of God."

We have this bias because the human brain has evolved to develop a sense of control over the world or at least over what happens to us. We become frightened when circumstances beyond our control affect us. When we witness a sudden, unexpected, or traumatic event, our natural response is to distance ourselves emotionally from the event by asserting that it all could have been prevented.

Consequently, jurors will focus on what the victim could have done to prevent the outcome rather than the actual cause of what happened. For example, in birth trauma cases, jurors can hold the mother more responsible for a bad outcome than the medical staff who actually inflicted the harm on her baby. Jurors will assert, "She shouldn't have missed the last prenatal visit," or "She should have left for the hospital earlier, even if she was told by the nurse to wait." It's easier to blame the mother than think that the medical people we have to rely on can make such a terrible mistake.

You have to alert jurors to this bias and how it can obscure what a plaintiff could have done or didn't do. You must make the distinction between prevention and causality. Jurors find it reassuring to their own sense of control by explaining a tragedy in a hierarchy of attribution: the plaintiff could/should have avoided it, God decided it and, lastly, the defendant doctor/police officer/etc. was negligent.

This sense of control must be addressed so that the attorney can circumscribe the acts of negligence to the individual defendant and a verdict against them as being a vehicle to reassure control.

There's a natural tendency to blame the victim and reassure ourselves that we would have avoided the same outcome. The more traumatic the injuries, the greater the tendency. You must alert jurors to this bias during your voir dire. Here's an example of this technique:

When I first learned of what happened, I was upset and felt bad for my client. Then I started thinking about what if that had happened to me or a family member— and something strange happened. I stopped focusing on what actually happened and what caused it to happen and started thinking of ways my client could have avoided it. Pretty soon what I "could have done" became what I "would have done" and then what "should have been done" to avoid the collision. That's how our emotions can create a bias.

I started to think, "What if he had done this instead, or that, or maybe never even left home that day ..." When I started to think about it, I'm pretty sure I would have never considered doing any of those things beforehand. I am an all-pro Monday morning quarterback.

Does anybody else do that when they hear about something really bad happening to someone? Does anyone else start doing a little Monday morning quarterbacking?

We all do it because that's how we reassure ourselves that it couldn't happen to us. It's a normal reaction.

But can you understand how our natural reaction can be unfair or a problem in this case? The law instructs us to consider whether the plaintiff did 'what is reasonable' to avoid an injury. It doesn't instruct us to consider whether the plaintiff did everything possible to avoid an injury. It was hard for me to distinguish between those two standards, and I'm a lawyer! Is there anyone here who thinks it would be hard to focus on what caused an accident rather than how the plaintiff could have avoided it?

Before you can effectively voir dire on this question, you have to reflect on your own reactions. If it's in the back of your mind that your client could have avoided the injury, this could be conveyed to the jury by your tone, manner, and questions. Sort it out, and then set to work helping jurors sort it out in their own minds. It's critical that you help jurors recognize and understand this bias during voir dire.

In cases of comparative negligence, it's also crucial to frame the issue carefully. It's not a matter of what could have been done by the plaintiff. Instead, the jury must understand that the defendant has to prove that what the plaintiff did or didn't do was not a reasonable response.

Jury Selection Strategies

While one purpose of voir dire is to identify jurors to deselect, the other purpose is to get a sense of how your jury will be structured. If you accept the idea that trials are a social process, then you already understand that jury deliberations are definitely a social process. As you consider the responses of a juror to voir dire questions and the quality of the interaction, you should also consider how that juror might be able to work with the other jurors. Which jurors are likely to form coalitions or defer to others? Who will lead or influence the jury, and who is likely to be a weak follower? Who are the coalition builders? Who are those likely to compromise? Which jurors are likely to resonate with the themes and evidence of the trial? These questions should affect your tactics in selection.

For example, you may have a juror who very likely won't support your case. If they were going to be the sole arbiter, you'd pass on this individual. However, if they are a passive individual in a group that has some strong jurors who are likely to be favorable to your cause, you might consider passing on a strike. They very likely will form a coalition with a strong plaintiff juror, and you'll save strikes for stronger opponents.

Pretrial research is also useful. It will give you a sense of which types of evidence to emphasize to persuade certain types of people. Research allows flexibility and gives you a good sense of how to work with jurors in your pool.

Still, you should voir dire every juror adequately. No amount of research should convince you to base your decision on a model profile alone. You simply can't control for all the life experiences of a juror. All jury research is based on a sample and is as valid and robust as the methodology and data analysis.

The most important tool is your own emotional acuity (your gut instincts) fleshed out and understood in the framework of the research but above all else based on the quality of the interaction with the person sitting in front of you in that jury box. Jury selection research and tools such as polling, mock trials, and handwriting analysis develop profiles based on structural characteristics such as demographics or characteristic writing styles. They have a predictive value in aggregate, but the individual in the jury box is less an aggregate of a group than they are of their life experiences, and those individual differences can be significant.

When I'm working with an emotionally astute attorney, I tend to trust their instincts over my own research when the two conflict. If we have a different sense of a juror, we discuss it. In those rare cases when the conflict is not resolved, we go with their instinct. The attorney must feel comfortable with his jurors, so even if their discomfort with a specific juror is not understood, it hardly matters. Here are a couple of other things to keep in mind:

- If the juror is a strong leader and you can't be certain if they are favorably disposed to your case, deselect them. Strong leaders can exert control over any group dynamics over time and cause a deliberation to flare out into unpredictable directions.
- Jurors who have had similar trauma or damages as the plaintiff are often adverse jurors. For example, an emergency room nurse might seem like someone who can understand the injuries and damages of the plaintiff. However, nurses often have to overcome their emotions to function in their jobs, and they struggle to suspend that emotional defense, which can make them unsympathetic to your client. Jurors are unlikely to suspend their own emotional defenses in response to a similar trauma.

Final Thoughts: Comfort and Challenge

Attorneys are trained from the first days of law school to rely on logic, intellect, and rhetorical constructions. That way of thinking is not always helpful in the courtroom. Instead, I have urged many of the attorneys I've worked with over the years to adopt a balance between comfort and challenge. In other words, they have to challenge themselves to take uncomfortable risks- being authentic and vulnerable in front of a jury, for instance- but not so uncomfortable that what they try to communicate is lost. If your vulnerability and your openness about your feelings and reactions is forced, you come across as phony and your behavior as contrived.

At the same time, your ability to know what you're feeling and why is an essential skill.

Some attorneys are drawn to law because it emphasizes logic and intellect and meshes with their own psychological preferences and defenses. They face all emotional challenges with logic and intellect. But learning the comfort-and-challenge approach, though challenging, can be personally and professionally rewarding. I know numerous attorneys who had the courage to take this risk and benefited immeasurably.

Key Takeaways
- Juries struggle to set a dollar figure for noneconomic damages like pain and suffering. We all experience misfortune and we're rarely compensated for it. But you must remind a jury—more than once, too—that the legal system requires fair compensation. Justice is measured by compensation and it's the only mechanism available to a jury.
- Attorneys often underestimate the monetary value of damages. Address your own biases about compensation before arguing your case before a jury. Never apologize for the amount of money you're seeking for your client. If you're worried the compensation you seek will alienate a jury you may have a bias that you must set aside to understand your client's pain and suffering.
- Never discuss a specific monetary amount during voir dire. Juries don't yet understand the meaning of your case, so the amount you set will become the filter through which jurors evaluate each piece of evidence. As a result, your evidence won't build up over the trial and become a powerful measure of what your client endured. Instead, each piece of evidence will be devalued as jurors measure it against the total compensation you've requested. Full compensation shouldn't be measured until all the evidence is presented and you've told the full story of your client's pain and suffering.
- Alert jurors to the natural "blame the victim" bias we all have. Warn them about the human tendency to believe the plaintiff could have done *something* to avoid the outcome. The jury must understand that the defendant has to prove any claim that the plaintiff shares the blame for the accident.

Chapter Four:

Opening Statements

If you succeed in voir dire, the jury trusts you. They understand you to be honest and forthright. Now they want to hear what you have to say. They want to know why they are here, why they should care about your case, and what they are supposed to do about delivering justice. Jurors are sacrificing their time and money, and they don't want to hear a legal lecture on the burden of proof or the elements to be proven. They don't want to hear about "roadmaps" or other theories. They want to hear the case.

Your opening statement is your best opportunity to tell them the story of your case and draw them into it. And the best way to do that is to get to the story right away.

If voir dire laid the foundation for your case, your opening statement provides the framework. It's not a simple recitation of the facts. Instead, it's your first opportunity to establish the *meaning* of the case. You have to describe what happened, why it happened, and how it happened, but most importantly it has to describe what these events mean, to your client, usually, but also, at times, to broader society.

Your story must have scope. It must have weight. It must be memorable, with the archetypal qualities of heroes and villains and tragedy and redemption. It's a story, and the best attorneys bring the jury into the story as pivotal participants in the narrative. They compel jurors to see themselves as the authors of the ending of this tale. If you tell the story well and convey the meaning, they are more than eager to step up and complete the narrative in the only way that makes sense- with justice for your client. Thus, there are two essential process goals with your opening statement:

- To provide and persuade the jurors to adopt your framework for understanding the issues in the case and then the meaning and significance of the evidence.
- To encourage jurors to become involved and invested in the outcome of the case.

Avoid the mistake many lawyers make of stuffing their opening statements with heavy facts and evidence. The jury must have a sense of the big picture and over-loading the opening with evidence is describing the trees, not the forest. You must describe the forest first. Facts do not necessarily communicate meaning or clarity; a fact-heavy opening will more often confuse jurors and obscure the narrative you want them to embrace and take authorship of.

Getting Started

The first step in constructing your narrative is to ask yourself, "What really happened here?" You must tell the story of your client so the juror understands the issues and significant evidence. What happened to the plaintiff, how were they affected by the incident, and what must be done for them to make it right? In this sense, the story has to transcend the simple contours of evidence. Who is this person? What kind of life did they lead? Where in their life did the event suddenly intrude and disrupt, and how has that disruption left them?

We've talked several times about the "meaning" of a case, and by now, you understand what that term refers to. It's the significance of the event- the way it irrevocably bent the arc of someone's life. But the meaning of a case can also encompass the significance it has to the larger world, lessons that are applicable to every human being, such as the notion of right versus wrong. Meaning is not just a philosophical or narrative construct; it's an essential tool in the brain's effort to process and precipitate action. The importance of meaning seems to be hardwired into the brain through evolution.

According to socio-biologists, it provides the mind with a working construct of the outside world and evokes a sense of control, predictability, and simplicity. Meaning helps us organize all the sensory information flooding the brain at any given moment to form an impression of what's happening. Thus, a good opening should conform to the natural arc of the mind. The simplest explanations are usually the most persuasive because they create order and predictability.

If you don't provide the meaning, jurors will supply their own, and their biases are likely to adversely affect your case. In mock trials, for example, jurors often summarize a case in terms of meaning rather than verdicts. They'll say the case was "all about money" or that "the plaintiff just wants to blame someone else for their mistakes." They won't tell you, "There was not enough evidence that the defendant was negligent." Instead, they make a judgment based on their understanding of the meaning of the case.

Exaggerating the meaning of your case to jurors can undermine credibility and reduce your damage verdicts. Don't reach for meaning- find the meaning. Some cases will involve issues and verdicts that will have implications for all of society (such as assisted suicide in the Jack Kervorkian cases), while others involve more personal issues, such as the meaning of a mother losing her baby to negligence. Some cases might change social policy while other cases might change the world of a family. But every case is important, just as one act of personal kindness is just as meaningful as creating a social movement. Justice is unaffected by scale, and scale is irrelevant to justice. Justice is always an important outcome, and doing justice is an experience and a privilege most people never have an opportunity to do. You define that opportunity for jurors with your story.

Presenting a rich and compelling opening statement does not involve using an argument to communicate meaning. Instead, use meaning to organize facts. Focus on how the evidence leads to truth. Don't try to create a cause or crusade where none exists, and avoid injecting more meaning into a case than it deserves. Instead, help jurors understand the meaning of the evidence for the client and why justice matters in a case that might at first seem remote or irrelevant to their own lives. The most effective stories about our clients are rooted in a compassionate and empathetic understanding of what happened to them, and the story is told in a way that gives meaning and relevance to jurors. Constructing openings is not dissimilar to writing a good story. The most successful trial attorneys are invariably good storytellers.

Using Introspection

Attorneys are accustomed to categorizing cases according to the guiding laws- products, medical malpractice, civil rights, and so on. This is about as descriptive as saying a story is fiction, non-fiction, romance, or biography. For example, some attorneys might describe their case as a legal box and the evidence as the details within it in the following manner: "This is an auto-negligence case, this is what the negligent driver did, these are the damages." However, this ignores the human story and the significance of the trauma to the victim. While most of us might say a rock is a rock, a geologist would see many distinctions, a long history, and a story behind every outcropping. The attorney must be like the geologist. It is not just a matter of having the legal insights and the facts of a case. It is also a matter of taking the time to realize what is present in every case and then how to form the story and tell it in a way that persuades and inspires.

Gerry Spence told me (more than once) that the most valuable skill of any trial attorney is the capacity for introspection. That is certainly true if you are writing an opening statement. Take the time to reflect on the client's story and what meaning it holds for you. Once you find that meaning, you will have a sense of the meaning to jurors and how to communicate that meaning to them.

This is important work. Developing the story of your case will guide many subsequent decisions. Once you have your story, other tactical decisions flow from it, including:

- The order of witnesses

   (how can my witnesses and the witness order help tell the story?)

- The focus of testimony

   (what evidence helps tell the story and should be emphasized?)

- Development of demonstratives

   (what exhibits illustrate and reinforce the story?).

Once the story of your case emerges through reflection on the client and the facts, the outlines of your opening statement emerge. The themes, the evidence that will or will not be introduced at that time, and the form of justice demanded are woven into the narrative. A metamorphosis takes place: evidence fleshes out the story, the story reveals the meaning, and the meaning reveals the best evidence to present.

Think about how great literature works. It instructs and inspires us by imbuing the narrative events with shared significance. Your opening statement should strive for the same effect. Great openers, like great literature, speak to our shared experience and compel us to look at the world and human experience in a new light. There is no case that does not involve human beings and, therefore, a shared human experience. Even the most complex copyright cases or idiosyncratic cases involve shared experiences.

What case of tortious interference doesn't involve some of the most basic of human emotions and experiences such as greed, betrayal, dreams made and stolen? Every case has a story, and every story has a lesson. When you seek the meaning of a case to yourself, the story you find will be yours to tell and will be authentic as the result. It will draw jurors into the drama and create a personal investment in the outcome.

Plot, Characters, and Conflict

Every great opening statement story has a plot, characters, actions, and conflict. Every story has an antagonist and a protagonist, and themes that bind the characters and evidence in meaning. There are good guys and bad guys. Sometimes the bad guy is the defendant, sometimes the defendant's attorney, and sometimes an anonymous insurance executive in a corner office at corporate headquarters. There's always an injustice perpetrated or inflicted. It is never a matter of fate or "no one's fault."

The facts of a case may seem remote to the everyday experiences of jurors, but if you tell the story well, you give meaning to facts. Some of the best stories I have ever heard or read involved plots alien to my own experience or knowledge, or involved topics I previously thought too boring to pursue. Good storytellers blast those preconceptions out of the water.

For example, when I was twelve and growing up in poverty near downtown Detroit, I read Jack London's short story "To Build a Fire" as part of a school assignment. I could hardly relate to a story of a wilderness trek across the Yukon, especially one with no dialogue and only one character. But the story enthralled me and still inspires me fifty-five years later with its insights into how greed and fear can lead to impulsive decisions and disastrous consequences. Again, it is less about the specific circumstances of every case as it is the client's story that you recognize as the human story.

The plot of your opening statement story evolves from the facts as they affect the characters, but it is the meaning that compels involvement. There was a television series in the late fifties and early sixties called "Naked City" that told a different police story each week. Every episode wrapped a story of a human being around a lesson any viewer could use in their own life. The specific circumstances or the plot of each drama may have been unfamiliar to viewers, but they were not unfamiliar to the human story. The actions and reactions of the characters always communicated something about the common experience of humanity. And each episode ended with a narrator intoning, "There are eight million stories in the Naked City. This has been one of them."

The best opening statement stories have not only a central conflict but a conflict that escalates over the course of the story. I worked on a case involving the construction of a huge auto plant in Indiana. The company had a cultural emphasis on getting things done on schedule, and that preoccupation led to some construction shortcuts which led in turn to our client suffering traumatic brain injury when a piece of quickly installed equipment collapsed. At trial, we mapped out the sequence of mistakes that led to the accident and we successfully created a sense with the jury that this accident was inevitable, even predictable. This wasn't an act of God but an act of negligence, and our client paid the price. That element of the story- that the accident was predictable and preventable- was consistent with what our brains want to believe and want to see the world, and the jury found in favor of the plaintiff.

Other Story Elements

Your story needs other components as well. There is a sequence of events that lead to a conflict, epiphany, or tragic ending. The story can embrace universal archetypes or themes, such as trust and betrayal, sin and redemption, or killing the golden goose. Some themes are universal; they are resonant with listeners in every culture or epoch. Psychotherapist Carl Jung speculated that all humans share a consciousness of these archetypes. The mythologist Joseph Campbell identified these types to include the "tragic hero," "sin and redemption," and "the man behind the curtain." The Star Wars series of movies exploited the archetype of the rogue turned hero. Archetypes provide familiar meaning, and the search for meaning is a human trait that seems to be universal.

What your story lacks in the telling, of course, is some final resolution of the central conflicts. Remember, finding meaning engenders the reassurance of understanding, control, and predictability. It also converts jurors from being mere agents awarding money for someone's injury to being crusaders righting a wrong and rectifying someone's unnecessary pain. As the storyteller, you invite jurors to play this part in the drama. They will provide the resolution. Only the jury can provide the denouement your tale cries out for. If you've done your job well, jurors will accept the responsibility and design an appropriate coda when the time comes.

The traumatic element of your story also must be carefully framed. It can't be portrayed as random or capricious but as predictable and preventable. At the same time, it must retain a quality of the unexpected. Let me explain. Jurors will resist the idea that the trauma suffered by the plaintiff could have happened to them. They want to believe that they would have seen the car coming and would have avoided it. They will believe that they never would have put themselves in the same situation that the plaintiff encountered. To believe otherwise is to accept a world without control or predictability, and the human mind vigorously repels that notion. People become anxious when their world seems unpredictable or random, and a common defensive reaction is to label the event and damages as "an act of God." They abandon any sense of control or responsibility and attribute the results to fate.

That way of thinking will dramatically affect the plaintiff's case, so it's imperative that you convince the jury that this accident was not the result of pure chance but the predictable and preventable result of the defendants' recklessness. Geoffrey Fieger, for instance, would always remind jurors that, "This accident was not an act of God. It was an act of negligence, and it was one hundred percent predictable, and one hundred percent preventable." This approach never fails to reassure jurors that their world remains orderly and that they have an obligation to deal with the individual (the defendant) who carelessly disrupted that order.

Keep in mind, too, that simple explanations are the most persuasive. A common mistake attorneys make is getting "lost in the weeds." In an effort to show the strength and scope of their case, they present so much detail that the core meaning of the case is lost or forgotten. If the story gets too involved and any elements seem capricious or arbitrary, then jurors will find a simpler explanation that is reassuring to them. Usually, that explanation won't help the plaintiff's case.

So, for your opening statement, present the best evidence that supports your story (what happened), provide a simple explanation (how it happened), a clear meaning (why it happened), and the remedy (what should happen now). A simple, credible explanation makes the case less challenging emotionally for jurors; it satisfies their innate preference for control, predictability, and preventability. If the world, through the issues of this case, can remain predictable and tragedies can be prevented, jurors are more likely to find the defendant negligent.

Some cases involving multiple defendants or multiple acts of negligence are complex, but it's crucial that you keep your story simple and linear. Avoid diversions into side issues, and present only evidence that leads jurors directly to the conclusion you want them to reach. The sequence of evidence should flow clearly to each defendant and each act of negligence and damage. You want the jury to sense the conclusion of your story before you even get to it.

As you reflect on "what really happened here," continually work to simplify and reduce your basic message. You should be able to describe even a complex case in just a few sentences. Of course, your opening statement will be longer than a few sentences, in most cases, but its central message should remain straightforward and succinct. If you don't keep it simple and concise, your story will confuse the jury, obscure the meaning, and prompt jurors to fall back to their own simple explanation (which isn't likely to help your case).

Crafting Your Story

The shape of the story you tell in your opening statement forms around the answers to a series of key questions:
- What was done to my client?
- Who did it, how, and why?
- How was my client affected?
- What must the jury do to ensure justice in this case?

The facts of the case are important but focus on the facts that imbue the story with meaning. For example, if you say, "The defendant ran a red light," that's a fact. If you say, "The defendant ran a red light because they were distracted," that's an explanation. But if you say, "The defendant was distracted while texting his girlfriend, causing a predictable and preventable collision that crushed the defendant and destroyed his life," you're using facts to give meaning to the circumstances.

As the meaning of the case takes shape in your mind, it's crucial that you search for your own understanding of what happened to your client. Try to understand not only what has happened to the client but also how they experienced it, and what it means to them. An attorney with such an understanding of their case has compassion and passion for the case. When you find the meaning of a case to you, then your representation of the case will be more authentic. The lesson you personally glean from the case is very likely the message you need to give to the jury through the opening. The themes of the client's story are truths, or lessons, that resonate with our own experiences, no matter what the facts of the case may be. Jurors may not identify with the circumstances or the client until you explain how it resonates with the human condition.

For example, a juror may not relate to the technical nuances of engineering schematics in a complex copyright infringement case, but they can certainly understand how it feels to have something important stolen from them. Most jurors will never experience damage due to medical negligence in a birth trauma case, but they will have the experience of being betrayed by someone they needed and trusted. They'll relate to the vulnerability of an infant.

You must ask yourself: What is the lesson here for jurors? What aspects of the case could anyone relate to? What evidence best communicates and confirms the meaning jurors can draw from the case? What witnesses best tell the story? What is the best order of witnesses to tell the story most effectively? To craft your client's story in a way that will resonate with jurors, their trauma must be characterized in a way that gives it a universal, existential quality. For example, losing a career or the ability to work may mean more to your client than financial damage. Some people define who they are as human beings by the work they do, thus this loss is not just financial, it undermines their self-belief.

The real significance of damages is found in an understanding of what that damage means to that person, and *that* evokes empathy, compassion, and actions. For example, hearing about another person's loss of a loved one causes us to pause to consider what it would mean to us to experience the same (and might prompt an overdue call to a parent or child). Considering the context of a client's damages provides an understanding of the true significance of their suffering.

Telling a Persuasive Story

The story you tell must have facts, timelines, and meaning, but it must also be told persuasively. This doesn't mean you should exaggerate or distort the facts to create a more entertaining or compelling story. People are persuaded by coherence, simplicity, shared understanding, and personal meaning, so your story must draw jurors into involvement by convincing them to understand the case the way you understand it. The best way to do that is by unveiling what this case teaches us all about life.

A good story starts with a strong, simple narrative. Use an active voice so it's clear who is acting and what they are doing. Pay attention to the pace of your story. Vary the length of your sentences and use vivid language instead of vague or empty constructions. For instance, instead of saying someone "suffered a torn ligament," say "their ligament was torn apart." Allow your delivery to quicken and your sentences to tighten when you reach the dramatic moments of the story. Write your opening statement ahead of time, and periodically read it aloud. Reading it aloud will help you notice awkward phrases, missing words, or places where the pace bogs down and your tale loses its urgency. Here are some other ideas for structuring your story:

Invite Jurors to Solve a Mystery

Create an opening with a mystery that leads jurors to believe they know the truth before you have suggested it to them. When jurors feel they've discovered the truth and "solved the mystery," they will be more persuaded and committed to a verdict. If you have constructed the story effectively, jurors will feel like the solution is theirs and they have a stake in following through to resolution (and justice for your client).

Medical malpractice cases lend themselves to this approach. Who contributed to the plaintiff's mistreatment and why? Mysteries recruit jurors to participate in the process of sorting out who the culprits were and what role they played. The process gives jurors ownership over the conclusions of the story. Mysteries create doubt about the obvious and allies with the natural skepticism of jurors in civil cases. For example:

When I first heard of the case, I thought I had enough information to know the truth. The defendant ran a traffic light and hit the plaintiff. At that point, it was just a matter of how badly the plaintiff was injured and what had to be done to make it right. But the more evidence I learned, the more a mystery emerged. Why was the plaintiff stashed in a hospital hallway without medical attention for four hours? Why hadn't doctors in the ER immediately ordered a chest X-ray that would have detected my client's hemothorax? As the questions mounted, I realized there was more to my client's suffering than we previously thought. Maybe you will have the same experience when you hear this evidence and together we can discover the real truth and do real justice.

In short, start with an important incident and ask, "How did this happen?" Jurors will try to figure the answer out from the evidence you present as the story unfolds. By the end of the opening, jurors will feel that the explanation is partly theirs.

Put Jurors in the Story

Tell the story from the point of view of a bystander. This will put each juror on the scene as an actual participant, making the event more vivid and compelling in their mind. Recruit them as partners in uncovering a mystery and discovering the truth, or as a participant or witness who is drawn into the tragedy.

Filter in details ("It was a sunny, warm morning") to help the jurors feel like they are on the scene. Remember to assert order and predictability to ease the jury's anxiety or fear about the randomness of the trauma. Remind them: "This was not an act of God; it was an act of negligence," or "This was one hundred percent predictable, and one hundred percent preventable." This will discourage them from falling back to some other interpretation that eases their apprehension but doesn't help your client's case.

Highlight the Importance of the Jury's Role

Jurors have put their lives and jobs on hold to hear this case, so they want to believe your case has significance and that their participation will be valued and essential. Tell the story in a way that captures their interests and elevates their role in the outcome. Along the same lines, don't waste a moment of the jury's time. Drive your story forward and get to the meaning as quickly as possible. Research tells us that seven to ten minutes is all you have in public speaking to capture interest. An hour is usually the limit of adult focus. Don't waste that time discussing the type of case or explaining legal processes.

For example, consider this brief introduction, which builds a bridge from voir dire to opening statement:

I want to thank you all once again for serving as jurors. I know it is a sacrifice for you and I will respect that sacrifice by presenting the case as efficiently as possible. I also think you will also find that being here today is an opportunity to do something that very few people get to do in life: an opportunity to create justice. I think that your service and verdict in this case will be something you will look back to in years as something you can be proud of doing—not just for doing your duty but to right a wrong. So, let me tell you why you are here today, this is what happened and why we need your help ...

Keep It Simple

Craft a story with a beginning, middle, and end, with each part flowing cleanly from the previous section. This kind of flow connects the evidence like dots and conveys parsimony and linearity- two key elements of persuasion. Remember, evidence leads to a story, a story to meaning, and meaning to justice. Mention only the evidence that will undergird your simple narrative. Once you embed that storyline in your opening, it's easier for jurors to understand any side issues that come up during the trial.

Avoid analogies. Jurors will focus on understanding the analogy, shifting their brain's focus from emotional involvement to intellectualizing. Instead, appeal to the jurors' common sense. If you're tempted to use an analogy, it usually means you haven't sufficiently boiled down your explanation and meaning enough.

Keeping your story linear and direct allows you to develop a recurring theme. For instance, a recurring theme in a medical malpractice case might be a careless doctor who betrayed the trust of his patient. Themes help identify the meaning of the case and increase jurors' emotional investment in the outcome. Evidence can be tied to the theme, and you can refer back to a theme like a trial mantra, thoroughly embedding it in the jurors' minds. Sometimes there is more than one theme; in the medical malpractice example, additional themes might include the hospital administration's efforts to cover up negligence or to victimize the patient a second time by trying to blame them for the trauma. Look for broad, simple themes, and remind the jurors of them throughout the trial as you introduce evidence.

Frame the Case with the Right Emphasis

For example, if you represent a victim of police brutality, focus on the excessive reaction instead of the incident that triggered the reaction. Done well, an initial reaction of "Well, no wonder the cop drew his gun" gives way to "I could see why they felt the need to restrain the guy, but, my God, why did they have to do that to him?" Here's an example:

Mr. Bennett stole two packages of hamburger from Johnson Grocery. He knew it was wrong, and when Officer Johnson grabbed him, Mr. Bennett broke free and ran. He ran down a side street, and when he was caught a few minutes later, he offered no resistance. He was out of breath and bent over trying to catch his breath when Officer Johnson approached him. Seconds later, Mr. Bennett was on the ground, bleeding. His leg was broken. Four bones in his face were fractured. By the time a second patrol car arrived three minutes later, Mr. Bennett was unconscious, his skull fractured. Despite the heroic efforts of paramedics, Johnson died en route to the hospital. He was killed because he broke loose from a police officer and ran away after stealing $10 worth of meat.

Mr. Bennett was wrong to steal the meat but the police were wrong too. Their job is to catch the "bad" guy and take him to jail, not to be the judge, jury, and executioner. Ten dollars' worth of hamburgers meant Mr. Bennett would be denied the same constitutional rights we all share—including the right to a fair trial and to equal justice. The evidence will prove that his beating and death were violations of our constitutional rights, and it was wrong. That's why we are here.

In framing the story, carefully select your words. For example, plaintiff attorneys in an auto negligence case often mistakenly describe the incident as an "accident" rather than as a "collision" or "crash." An "accident" suggests to most people that the incident was unavoidable and that no one is to blame—not the message you typically want to send. Likewise, avoid technical terms that can sanitize the brutal reality. For example, saying a child died from slowly becoming "hypoxic" will have less effect on jurors than saying the child "slowly suffocated."

Avoid Using Clinical Language or Legalese

You might use terminology when discussing the case with legal or medical experts but clinical language will confuse jurors and could prevent them from seeing the underlying meaning of the case. Use the language jurors use. Online tools like hemmingwayapp.com will help keep your messages bold and clear. Aim for simple language at no higher than an eighth-grade level.

Discussing legal principles in your opening will detract from your story. For instance, if you discuss the burden of proof in your opening statement, this may signal to jurors that you lack confidence in your case. If you tell them that you only need to prove a "tiny bit" more than the defendant to win, jurors might think the trial will be a close call. Save the burden of proof discussion for the closing. Instead, focus on your absolute commitment to right a wrong and secure justice for your client. Jurors are inspired by their sense of right and wrong, not the letter of the law.

If you must discuss the elements to be proven, do it at the end of your opening. Introduce them as a means of doing justice rather than as an apology about the burden of proof or legal argument. Use the elements to summarize the meaning of the evidence to the verdict the jurors will decide.

Cite the evidence as an example of the element. For example, "The collision was so violent that it literally ripped the aorta from her heart, and she bled to death in a few minutes. That is the definition of causation- proximate cause. The collision ripped the aorta causing her to bleed to death. The cause of death (proximate cause) was…"

Don't Rely Too Much on the Reptile Brain Trial Strategy

Authors David Ball and Don C. Keenan introduced this approach in 2009, and countless plaintiff attorneys have used it since. The strategy involves getting jurors to see defendants as immediate threats to society, triggering a part of the juror's brain that governs instincts. Jurors see the danger posed by the defendant and innately desire to protect themselves and their community from that harm. The so-called reptile brain controls such life functions as hunger and breathing and primitive fight or flight survival instincts. Once we perceive a threat to our safety and activate this portion of the brain, logic and reason have trouble prevailing. Keenan and Ball recommend several approaches to activate these survival instincts, but the core strategy is to focus on danger and community safety. This is a limited understanding of how the mind comes to perceive the "rules" and the relevance of those rules to the issues in the case. Autonomic responses are perceptual and reflexive, not cognitive. For those "reptilian" responses to become a verdict it is essential to understand the role of affective information processing and the social nature of the trial process.

After you establish the danger, the key is convincing jurors they are the only people in a position to stop the threat. To do that, they need to provide compensation, deliver justice to the plaintiff, and send a powerful message to the defendant. The Reptile Theory is an effective framing for some cases but not all, and there is some legal nuance involved. You have to craft any argument not as an implicit encouragement to reach a "send a message" verdict. It is more effective to use your own reactions and thought processes on the evidence to suggest how to frame the story. Justice is vital to the survival of civil society, but it's not a survival imperative.

Frame Bad Evidence

The defendant's evidence can be used against them. For instance, if the defense brings up the plaintiff's difficult past, such as a criminal history, don't ignore it. Coopt it in your opening. Acknowledge that criminal history and weave it into the inspiring story of your client's fall and redemption: just as they were realizing their dream and overcoming their past, your client encountered the defendant and their dream was shattered.

***

Surveillance video is often very damaging to a damage case because the evidence in the video is often ambiguous – very rarely do they ever reveal the "aha" evidence. The reason why they almost always hurt the plaintiff's case is because the jurors project their biases to interpret the video. Plaintiffs must use that evidence in their case if the video evidence cannot be excluded. Co-opt the video evidence by having your damage expert review it and use it during their testimony to illustrate evidence of injuries too subtle for jurors to discern, or using the techniques learned in therapy. Use lay witnesses to put the video in context and perspective.

After thirty years and hundreds of cases, I've never seen "bad stuff" that could not be turned into an asset at trial. Negotiators call this process an "accusation audit." In your opening, you freely label any potentially damaging information about your client and reframe it to help establish the meaning of the case. Even a weak or inadequate explanation of "bad stuff" is better than failing to discuss it all in your opening statement. Allowing the defense to introduce it will undermine the credibility and trust you've worked so hard to establish with the jury.

Discussing Money Damages

As we discussed in the last chapter, you should introduce the idea that monetary damages are the only justice allowed to jurors. However, you should only use general terms and amounts. Asking for specific amounts will cause jurors to judge damage evidence in terms of whether it is worth the amount being requested. They will evaluate damage evidence piecemeal rather than as a collective impact. They will also be inclined to evaluate each element of damages in terms of dollar amount rather than in terms of the impact it had on the plaintiff.

If you tell the jury during the opening that you will ask for fifty million dollars at the end of the trial, jurors will react. No juror has ever seen fifty million dollars, and certainly, no one has ever been offered that much money. They have no context to understand that amount of money, except their own experience of never seeing that amount.

So instead of citing a specific amount, suggest in your opening that damages are such that a significant amount of money will be required to do justice. Keep jurors focused on the impact and meaning of the damages. Jurors will still react to the amount of money at closing, but their reaction will be filtered through their full understanding of both the damages and the meaning of the case. Damage evidence should accumulate like the stones piled on Giles Corey, the farmer who was pressed to death for refusing to enter a plea to the charge of witchcraft in the play "The Crucible." Each stone might not seem like much, but by the end of the trial, the cumulative weight of all the damages will crush jurors' biases against money damages.

Using Demonstratives

I have bias regarding the use of technology in trials, but I am no Ted Kaczynski. I'm not a big fan of using PowerPoints during the opening statement. Here's why:

- PowerPoints often make the opening feel scripted and overproduced. It feels like a classroom session to jurors and many will disengage. But telling your client's story in your own heartfelt words draws them in like a good campfire story.
- The jurors' mental images are typically more disturbing than the actual damage. Tell your story and let the jurors' imaginations fill in the details. The image they create themselves will be far more vivid and memorable than a slide in a PowerPoint deck.
- The time you spend preparing a PowerPoint robs from the time you must spend examining your own heart and mind in search of the true story and the case's meaning. If *you* don't understand the meaning, the jury won't either. As a result, the PowerPoint tends to be sterile, incoherent, and certainly less heartfelt and compelling than a strong story well told. Hearing and then seeing is the optimal sequence for learning.
- There are inevitable technological glitches. These not only disrupt the flow of your story but they make jurors anxious and frustrated, making them unreceptive to your message. A botched PowerPoint hurts the trust and credibility you need to establish with a jury. Even worse is when the attorney encounters a technological failure and is unable to continue with the opening until the problem is fixed.
- Some believe younger jurors are video-driven and need visual stimulus to overcome their short attention spans. I don't believe this. The science of learning is well-established; excessive video exposure diminishes learning effectiveness. Too much visual stimulation distracts and fails to consolidate into our memories.
- Graphic damage demonstratives or exhibits should come after the context is established during the trial. Once the jury understands the client and the effect

of an injury to that client, then the demonstratives or exhibits become more effective. That said, the more a shocking picture or video is shown, the less impact it will have. Some images will offend more than they enlighten, and a juror's imagination of an injury will often be worse than the reality.

Despite my reservations, strategic use of technology can be powerful. Visuals can be particularly useful in complex product or financial cases. Low-tech demonstratives such as blow-ups of medical records, family photos, and the like can powerfully reinforce jurors' understanding and memory of the evidence. Animations can make technical processes understandable and simple, especially in product cases and environmental cases.

Key Takeaways

- Your opening statement should establish what happened, how, and when, but most importantly it should establish the *meaning* of the events that affected your client. How did it forever change the arc of their lives or have an impact on society at large?
- Tell a story—a story that has heroes, villains, and fateful circumstances. Ultimately, your opening argument should establish the role of the jurors. Be clear that they will be asked to set right the wrongs you describe.
- Jurors will resist the idea that your client's misfortune could ever befall them. That's human nature, and they'll want to hold your client responsible in some way. You must convince them that your client's injuries were predictable and preventable and caused by the defendant's recklessness.
- Keep your story simple and direct and discuss only the evidence that supports that version of events. Make the case easy for jurors to accept emotionally.
- Present your story as a mystery that allows jurors to realize "who did it" before you tell them. When jurors feel they've discovered the truth on their own, they become more committed to a verdict. Avoid words like "accident" (which suggests the mishap was not caused by anyone but was an act of God) and avoid jargon of any kind.
- Introduce monetary damages as the only means of justice available for jurors to mete out. Never discuss a precise dollar amount.

Chapter Five:

Witnesses

The case involved a man who had suffered a traumatic brain injury in a vehicle collision caused by another driver. The man's memory had been impaired, and the injury to his frontal lobe had affected his ability to learn new things and control his impulses and moods. Attorney Jennifer D'Amico wanted the man's wife to testify about how the accident had changed her husband.

The attorney had done her research and learned that TBI victims with this pattern of injury often have problems with anger and violence, whether from frustration about their impairments or because the damage itself precipitates rage without any external cue. She learned of a subtle symptom of TBI injuries that therapists call "the look", a wide eyed angry expression that preceded an angry outburst. We felt the wife's testimony was key to establishing the extent of the plaintiff's injuries, but when we interviewed her before her deposition, the woman seemed reluctant to tell the full story.

"The neuropsychological testing showed that he might have problems being impulsive and with mood swings," my attorney asked the wife. "Have you noticed any problems like these?" "No, not really," she said. "He gets frustrated sometimes, but…" Her voice trailed off and she looked away. The attorney waited a moment with the discomfort and then softened her tone of voice. "Does he ever get that look in his eyes? Do you know what I mean?"

The wife turned by to the attorney, looking a bit startled. "Yes," she said quietly. "You know what that means, don't you?" "Yes." "What does it mean for you?" "It means I have to get the kids and leave for a while." "You don't feel safe then?" the attorney asked. "No, it's not safe for us," the wife said, her eyes welling with tears. "I know he doesn't mean it ... It's just that he's changed so much." She began to sob.

The two had been high school sweethearts. They'd known each other for over twenty years. But after the accident, the man's personality changed. He didn't act the same; he could turn violent and physically abusive, and he'd never been that way before. The wife was reluctant to talk about it, partly because she hoped he would improve and partly because she was thinking of leaving him and felt like she would be deserting him. She felt trapped between guilt about divorcing him and guilt that she was exposing her children to abuse.

As the truth emerged, the pain poured out of her as fast as her tears. No one had asked about her experience with his injury before. But a little bit of knowledge, a couple of questions, and a lot of watching and listening to her allowed the true damages to emerge. Those damages were much more profound than anyone had suspected. We were able to find counseling and support for her and amended the complaint to include a consortium claim for her. The story reveals several crucial aspects of preparing witnesses to testify:

- It is often difficult for plaintiffs and witnesses who have suffered damage to articulate those damages. They have probably spent months, if not years trying to not think about it and to move on with their lives. They certainly made adaptations to life after the damage has been done. Those adaptations include emotional defenses that allow them to continue with their lives with as little emotional turmoil as possible, as well as dozens of physical adjustments that may seem so ordinary that they may not mention them. These emotional defenses include denial, minimization, and other means of not allowing the suffering to interfere with their day-to-day activities. They must walk a careful balance between feeling and coping, communicating and continuing. This means that your discussions with them about the damages must always consider those defenses and how they are affecting their perception and communication of the damages. The responsibility for disarming those defenses long enough to allow their pain to surface and be expressed.
- Preparing a witness does not mean scripting or rehearsing a witness. That approach will diminish the credibility and effectiveness of a witness. A scripted or rehearsed witness is not being authentic and therefore less credible and will stumble on cross-exam.

- You have to establish a relationship with witnesses. Learn about them and how they like to communicate and how to best communicate with them. This takes time. Like voir dire, it's a social process and first impressions are crucial to establishing a good relationship. Many witnesses become anxious thinking about testifying, and many are guarded or defensive. Some resent the intrusion in their lives and don't understand what to focus their testimony on. Family members of clients will have additional emotional issues that can hamper their full, honest testimony. However, if they feel comfortable with you, they can reveal information not previously known and will be willing to participate in the narrative you want to communicate.

How to Think About Witnesses

A witness' role is to provide evidence that supports the narrative you want to tell the jury. You will tell the story better than any witness, and your job is to make sure the witness understands which part of that story they will help provide and why it's important. The evidence they give supports and adds context to the narrative. They are confirming rather than constructing the story. The goal is for jurors to think, "Aha, I knew it!" rather than "Okay, what does that mean?"

The most effective witness not only understands the significance of their evidence to the essential case narrative but is able to testify concisely and coherently. They understand what the case is about and how their testimony fits in. They are not telling the story; they are confirming the story by sharing their evidence.

Since many witnesses are dealing with anxiety or emotional obstacles, one of your jobs is to lower their apprehension so you can increase their effectiveness. This will require you to learn about their history and life independent of the case. You can create a willing witness by communicating an interest in them as a person, respecting them, and demonstrating authentic kindness for them and what they are going through. Authenticity is just as important to witnesses as it is to jurors.

Another important aspect of helping a witness relax and testify effectively is mastering your own anxiety. Those of us that have been parents come to realize our children are often a better barometer of our own moods than we are sometimes. I remember vividly my education in this regard. As a graduate student, I was invited to be a speaker at a national conference on creating zero-fee treatment programs for indigent populations. One of my personal heroes, Dr. Harold Eist, was also invited. The idea of being on the same stage with such a magnificent person was both a source of pride and extraordinary anxiety that I would, as St. Augustine said, "experience humiliation as the surest route to humility."

I drove Dr. Eist and his wife to dinner that night and brought my son along with me. I was plenty nervous, and my anxiety worsened when my son started fidgeting and fussing. I tried not to show my growing irritation, but apparently, I wasn't doing such a great job. At one point, Dr. Eist leaned forward from the back seat and said, "It's amazing how children pick up on our anxiety before we do, isn't it?" Humility was another passenger then.

The same is true with witnesses, who are already anxious enough before testifying. If the attorney is anxious about their testimony, then it will translate to the witness. It might take the form of scripting the witness so they won't "misspeak," or too many reassurances that they will be fine. You should reduce your own anxiety before working with a witness, especially a lay witness. You must be able to believe that nothing they can say will harm the case or can't be remedied.

Once they are comfortable with you, help them get comfortable with the process. Most laypeople have never been in a courtroom, let alone as a witness, so the experience can be intimidating. Educate them on what to expect and reassure them. Describe the logistics, such as where to park, how to get to the courtroom, who to report to, and what to expect in terms of waiting to be called. Explain how they will be waiting in the hall, and that when they are called, they will go to the front of the courtroom and be sworn in. Take them through all the procedural things related to their testimony. Go over what to do when objections or other interruptions interfere with their testimony. Explain the difference between a deposition and trial testimony, and help them prepare for both. This will ease their anxiety about testifying at trial.

Another part of the preparation is helping them understand their role and testimony. Familiarize them with the process of testifying. You are not telling them the story and what to say as part of that story, but you are explaining why their testimony has significance to you and your understanding of what happened. This also keeps them focused during cross-examination. Witnesses rarely have a sense of how their testimony fits in with a case, so explain how their tree fits into the forest of the trial. They should understand what your questions will focus on so they can deliver clear, cogent, and effective testimony.

They may need to be reassured that there is no risk to them. Chat with them prior to their testimony or deposition. Having a conversation is less intimidating than an examination, and this will help them feel comfortable telling their story. It will also give you some insight into how to best question the witness when the time comes. You'll see their psychological defenses and get practice on removing those obstacles before the trial begins. Casual conversations like these also help witnesses expand on their perceptions and reactions. A relaxed witness is more likely to volunteer information.

Some attorneys coach their witnesses ("Always look at the jurors when you answer a question"), but I advise against stage directions. Your witness will be nervous enough and jurors might see that the eye contact from the witness is some kind of contrivance and become distrustful. Your witnesses' credibility will be based on how comfortable, confident, and consistent they are on the stand, and the best way to achieve that is through pretrial conversations.

During those conversations, you can help witnesses be clear and specific by asking questions and reflecting back to them what you hear them saying. Your response is not an attempt to put words in their mouth but instead to focus and clarify what they are telling you. They may choose to adopt your interpretation and use it during testimony, but it will be authentic.

You can also prepare them for cross-examination by building their confidence. That confidence comes from an understanding of how their testimony relates to the meaning of the case, and that focus and clarity cut down on confusion during cross-examination. You can also play devil's advocate with them and help them avoid some common mistakes, such as filling in memory gaps with speculation or responding defensively to contradictions in their testimony. The key is to tamp down any anxiety *you* have about their testimony; if you're nervous, the witness will be, too.

Understanding Your Witness

Some witnesses are traumatized by what they witnessed, and it's vital that you understand this. These witnesses need to feel like you are relating to them as an individual and not as a tool being used for the case or a suspect being interrogated. Listen to them and try to understand their experience. Always be alert for potential damage testimony. For example, witnesses to a traumatic event are often traumatized as well. Allowing them to experience and to relate that trauma will have an effect on the jurors' perception of the damages to the client.

As we learned in the case described at the beginning of this chapter, damage witnesses, especially family members, often resist sharing information because they are caught in an emotional bind of caring for a loved one at a cost to their own lives. This can create ambivalence, resentment, anger, and guilt. Identifying and understanding their experience first can be a key to getting the damage testimony you need. That knowledge can also help the witness better understand their own experience and free them from their own suffering.

This doesn't mean you should become a psychotherapist, but it does require you to have the empathy, compassion, and emotional acuity needed to establish trust. You must learn how to listen carefully and to read their nonverbal cues. When do they go silent and why? When should you press them to overcome their defenses and when should you back off those defenses?

The benefits of approaching the damage witness this way are not only a more complete sense of the damages but also the ability to elicit those damages when they testify at trial. In a conversation with a loved one about a terrible event they have suffered, we intuitively know when to ask questions and when to listen and when to just be quiet and be there. Try to develop and apply the same emotional acuity with your clients when talking about their damages.

Damage is in the Details

Often, the depth of damages is found in the smallest details of life. These are the minutiae that many may overlook or fail to testify about. We all make dozens of decisions every day that we never think twice about- getting up to pour a glass of water or reaching down to pick up a granddaughter. But a person suffering from chronic discomfort goes through a mental calculus of pain when considering these things. Getting up to use the restroom takes planning and courage. Turning around to see who's calling takes a calculated effort.

When establishing damages through witnesses, no detail is too trivial. Sometimes the details involve pain too difficult to articulate or too intimate to be accessible without prompting. However, jurors expect you to present the most profound effects of the damages and they weigh that damage against their own understanding and experiences. What they don't expect or appreciate is how the ordinary aspects of life that they all share with the client are affected. Here are two examples of how the ordinary becomes valued:

In one case in which an elderly woman was killed in an auto collision caused by another driver, the victim's elderly husband, who survived the crash, testified as to how the death affected him. After fifty-eight years of marriage, the synergy between the man and his wife had been so complete that the details were difficult to disentangle. Nothing felt right or normal, the man said. He felt a constant sense of "wrongness." Everything seemed to lack something. The man struggled to speak and to describe the depth of his loss and how much he missed his wife. Then the attorney asked, "How long was it before you replaced her pillowcase?" The old man paused, then began sobbing. Two years after her death he still hadn't changed her pillowcase because it smelled of her hair and that was all he had left. By then, several jurors were also crying with the man, and the judge had to dismiss the court for fifteen minutes to allow everyone to compose themselves.

Another case involved a strong, independent woman who had just retired from teaching after thirty years when she suffered a spinal injury in a rear-end collision. She had raised three children as a single mother and had been deprived by the accident of her chief pleasure in life: participating in a golf league and socializing at her country club. But none of the jurors golfed or belonged to a country club and they could not value the woman's loss. However, later in her testimony, the woman revealed an intimate and uncomfortable detail of her suffering; she could no longer bend enough to clean herself after using the toilet and had to depend on others to do this for her. It was embarrassing and humiliating for her and caused her to isolate herself socially. The emotion she expressed at being unable to do something that everyone on the jury could do without a second thought was much more evident than discussing golf, and the jury understood the context and profound effect it had on her emotionally as well as physically. Every juror could feel that embarrassment and humiliation, if not her pain, and understood the meaning of her suffering. The verdict was nine million dollars for the plaintiff, with seven and a half million dollars in noneconomic damages.

We'll discuss damages in more detail in a future chapter, but here are a few guidelines for examining a witness or client on damages:
- Understand the full range of damages possible, including the aftereffects of an injury. Not all damages are documented in medical records or diagnosed by treating physicians. Clients might see symptoms but attribute them to something else. They rarely want to consider that future problems will emerge, and doctors rarely discuss them.

- You, as the plaintiff's attorney, have to educate yourself on future problems stemming from the initial injury. For example, people who suffer traumatic brain injury often don't recognize their impairments or associate impairments with the injury. You have to be aware of these common, uncommon and potential consequences of the damage so that you can ask about them in court.
- Understand that you may have biases about damages and how the client expresses them. Some clients may seem overly dramatic while others remain stoic. Either way, your bias may compel you to downplay the damage and for others to do the same. However, if you're aware of that bias and hold it in check, your client will trust you and feel safe enough to reveal their pain.
- Put yourself in your client's shoes. This will help you develop an empathetic understanding of how your client was affected. It also puts damages into context—the client's context.

One example of understanding context was the case of a young woman who lost her first child due to negligence during the delivery. Someone who has never carried a baby to term may not understand that a mother's relationship with their baby begins long before birth and the loss of a relationship is much more profound than usually appreciated. To introduce that idea, the attorney asked the mother what her baby's favorite and least favorite foods were. She instantly responded that he loved Church's Fried Chicken but hated asparagus. After she ate asparagus, the baby would toss and turn in her womb, and she would have to rub him constantly to calm him down. She spoke about her baby as though he were already born, and her attachment to him was apparent. Mothers understand, but the context of their loss may not occur to the single male attorney unless he takes the time to understand his client before considering the effect of their damages.

Understanding an experience from the perspective of a witness can be helpful for any of the damage witnesses. An emotional reaction of a witness to an auto collision can communicate the violence and terror of the trauma to the people actually in the vehicles. Understanding how emotional defenses function can help you work through the resistance and hostility of a witness.

Uncovering Emotional Defenses

For example, in 1999, Geoffrey Fieger was hired by a shooting victim's family in a civil suit against Warner Bros.; Telepictures, a subsidiary of Warner Bros.; and *The Jenny Jones Show*. The case involved a 1995 episode of *The Jenny Jones Show* in which the victim, Scott Amedure, admitted to being a secret admirer of Jonathan Schmitz, who lived near him in Lake Orion, Michigan. Schmitz shot and killed Amedure three days later.

Schmitz had agreed to be on the show without knowing who his secret admirer would be but assumed that the person would be a woman. While waiting to be called on stage, Schmitz watched as Amedure revealed his attraction to Schmitz. Jones then encouraged Amedure to describe his fantasies about Schmitz, after which Schmitz was brought on stage. According to the *Washington Post*, Schmitz laughed about Amedure's admission and said he was "definitely heterosexual." Three days later, after Schmitz found what the New York Times later described as a "suggestive" note at his house, Schmitz bought a shotgun, confronted Amedure at Amedure's home, and shot Amedure twice in the chest, killing him. Schmitz immediately called 9-1-1 and confessed.

Amedure's family hired Geoff to sue Warner Bros, Telepictures, and *The Jenny Jones Show* for their ambush tactics and negligence that led to Amedure's death. We argued that Schmitz, who had been diagnosed with bipolar disorder and Grave's disease, had been caused to commit homicide when the show created an unpredictable situation without any consideration of the consequences. A psychiatrist serving as our expert witness testified that the show, in deceiving someone with mental illness, had committed "psychological assault and battery."

Schmitz would not have killed Amedure if the two had not been on the show, he said.

Ven Johnson was an associate attorney in the trial and was given the job of interviewing Schmitz's girlfriend, a key witness in the trial. Unfortunately, the girlfriend was not cooperative. She refused to talk to either side and was openly hostile to both parties. On the day she was scheduled to testify, Johnson approached me in the Oakland County Circuit Court cafeteria. He was uncharacteristically nonplussed. How, he wanted to know, was he supposed to approach this woman?

This case turned on our ability to establish that the show's deceitfulness and trickery had triggered Schmitz's "gay panic defense," a form of temporary insanity that caused Schmitz to believe he was acting in self-defense. (What kind of testimony could the girlfriend give that would help you establish this and establish the meaning of the case to jurors?) I glanced around the cafeteria and spotted the woman sitting alone across the room. (A brief physical description here would be great.)

We knew so little about her that it was impossible to determine the best way to question her. So I suggested to Ven that we simply try to engage her. He agreed. We walked over, and I introduced myself and Ven and asked if we could join her for a few minutes. She leveled her gaze at me for a moment, and then her face twisted into an angry, hateful expression. She pointed at me and then at Ven. "Fuck you," she said, "and fuck you. Go away."

This did not reassure Johnson, of course, and when we returned to our table, I could see he was utterly focused on the impending disaster of this woman's testimony. Nothing worries an attorney more than having no idea how a witness will testify. There are simply too many ways that the witness can undermine the case you're trying to build. So I steered Ven into a discussion about how anger is *a defense* as much as a *reaction* and how he could recognize an opening to reveal the emotion behind this woman's anger.

The woman's testimony began just as Ven feared it would, with the girlfriend giving pinched one-word answers or hostile responses. Then Ven asked how the woman had been informed of the murder. The woman paused and then looked down at her hands clenched in her lap. Johnson saw this and immediately changed the tone of his voice. Gently, he asked her, "What are you just feeling right now?"

The woman lifted her eyes to the courtroom and suddenly began sobbing. "How could they do this to people?" she wailed, making it clear that she was referring to the television show and its producers. "How can they do this to make money from this, from humiliating people like this? They've destroyed so many lives … for what? Why?"

There it was. Her anger was visceral, and it was clear what the source was- a heartless TV show that manipulated people for the pure shock value and the profits that come with that. The jury awarded the Amedure twenty-nine million dollars, and when I spoke with jurors after the trial, several of them told me that the girlfriend's testimony was the deciding factor that made the meaning of the case clear to them.

Fieger was also astute at understanding defenses and how to use them during testimony. One of the defenses in the trial was that Schmitz laughed when he realized that his "secret crush" was a man. His reaction showed that he couldn't have felt humiliated. After the first day of testifying, we observed that Ms. Jones tended to laugh nervously at times under withering cross-exam. The next day, Fieger waited for just the right moment and asked her, "I notice that you smile a lot when answering questions. Why is that? Do you think it's funny?" She took the bait and said, "I guess I smile when I am really uncomfortable." "That's right," Fieger thundered, "and that's exactly what Schmitz was doing when you ambushed him, wasn't it?" Ms. Jones looked at the jury and sat in the witness chair with a frozen smile that said it all.

Expert Witnesses

Post-trial interviews with jurors have also consistently shown that expert witnesses are most effective when they:

- **Are good teachers.** Jurors appreciate experts who use simple, understandable language. It also helps when the expert's testimony is consistent with jurors' common sense and experience.
- **Project a belief in themselves and in the case.** Most experts think it's crucial that they remain objective or dispassionate on the stand. They think this adds to their credibility; their statements are based on facts and are not altered by the fact they were hired by one side of a dispute.

But experts are more persuasive when they project a belief in the case (or at least an unshakable belief in their opinion) and an unwavering commitment to their opinion about it. They are not apathetic or indifferent to the case, and they don't entertain absurd defense hypotheticals. They don't necessarily advocate for the client or become argumentative, but they advocate for their opinion and how it affects the case. Jurors want to know whether the expert actually *believes* what they are saying and believes how the evidence reflects on the verdicts in the case.

Your expert's resume rarely makes a difference with jurors. In the jury's mind, experts are experts. A doctor from Harvard has no more credibility than a doctor who graduated from a state school. The only thing that matters is that communicate well to the jury and project a firm belief in your case.

The expert's fee also rarely makes a difference with jurors. They know experts get paid and most understand the fees are substantial. In over a hundred trials, I can think of only one or two occasions when an expert's astronomical fee had an impact, and that was because the expert's fee was far higher than other experts who testified.

Of course, you can point to the exorbitant fees paid by the defense as a sign of the true value of the damages to your client. An example is when an insurance company invests money in surveillance on your client rather than paying his hospital bills. They are willing to hire spies to dig up dirt on your client because the financial consequences of being held responsible are much more significant.

Managing Your Expert Witness

Experts must understand the case and their role in it, but as specialists, they should focus on evidence that is pertinent to their expertise. Think of it this way: they focus on the trees but are aware of the forest. In medical malpractice cases, for instance, they may explain that a given lab result means one thing in most cases but means something entirely different in the context of your client's case. They are not willing to concede the improbable alternative explanations given by the defense and aren't bashful about pointing out how absurd the defense's hypotheticals are to the plaintiff's overall case.

Regardless of whether they are a doctor, engineer, or forensic accountant, you must lead your experts to the context of the case. Ask them to review portions of the record that may be technically outside their area of expertise but nevertheless might have an impact on their opinion. Asking them how these other findings impact their opinion gets them more involved in the case overall and prepares them for cross-examination. Specialists must understand how their opinion on a narrow set of facts affects the case so that they are ready if the defense tries to twist the facts to undermine the truth during cross-examination.

You have to develop your relationship with your experts in much the same manner that you develop relationships with jurors. Experts are typically more familiar with the legal process than most, but it pays to learn how to communicate most effectively with them. In psychotherapy, we call it "allying with the defense." This means you take the time to understand how the expert sees themselves and the world so you can phrase questions that are consistent with their defenses.

For example, some experts appear to be arrogant and egotistical. But if you understand that these are defenses against an underlying fear of failure, it's easier to tolerate them and get the testimony you need. Understanding their defenses also makes it easier to increase their emotional investment in the outcome because they adopt the opinion on a more personal level. Understanding how they communicate will lead to better trial testimony. Understanding them as humans outside of the context of their being experts also increases your own comfort with each other at trial.

In preparing for one trial, our expert physician seemed to enjoy correcting or contradicting the attorney. It was a problem. If he were to exhibit this kind of passive-aggressive style in court, it would undermine our case. The attorney asked me to intervene and see what I could do to change the expert's approach. Rather than probing his attitudes about the attorney or the case, I decided to learn about him as a human being. I took him to breakfast and learned that he and I shared an affinity with the old Brooklyn Dodgers baseball. The Dodgers, led by Roy Campanella behind the plate and Carl Erskine, Don Newcombe, and Preacher Row on the mound, were the dominant team of the late forties and early fifties, and the doctor relaxed and became animated when I asked him what it was like to grow up in Brooklyn during those years, He talked about seeing Pee Wee Reese, Jackie Robinson, the joy of games at Ebbets Field. I tell you, we were both in our element.

From there, the conversation imperceptibly flowed into more personal matters, and I learned that the doctor was struggling a bit with his emotions. He was transitioning from a career in research and treatment to more forensic work, and it was raising existential questions in his mind. He seemed to feel like he was taking a step down from the lofty role he once played, and this was causing him to be condescending and contrary.

Later that day, we met with the attorney to go over the doctor's testimony. To pull him back to a time when the world was new and exciting still, I frequently made baseball references. This annoyed the attorney, I could see, but it kept the doctor in an accommodating, reverential frame of mind. Later that day, the doctor's testimony was superb—clear, easy to understand, and patient. None of the haughty imperiousness we'd seen earlier.

"It's like you used a Jedi mind trick on him," the attorney told me. No, it wasn't. It was stepping back when meeting resistance to understand the source of the resistance. After shedding the role of expert, expert witnesses are ultimately as fragile as any other human being.

The Order of Witnesses

I've witnessed many trials where witnesses are called in a disorderly rhythm that forces jurors to piece together the chronology from scraps of memory. We hear testimony on the plaintiff's injuries before we hear anything about the accident that caused the injuries. Sometimes, this is caused by the unpredictable availability of witnesses, but more often, it's the product of an attorney too lazy to accommodate the orderly way jurors prefer to think about a case.

The order of witnesses is an important strategic and tactical maneuver. You have already told the jury the basic structure of your story with your opening statement; now, use witnesses to provide the color and texture the story needs to be persuasive and compelling. Witnesses should follow the natural order of the story, and the testimony of one witness should flow directly from the preceding witness and into the testimony of the next. Each witness should pick up the narrative where the last witness left off. Done right, witnesses will deliver timely answers just as the questions are forming in the jurors' minds.

As I mentioned, jurors don't like this information to be out of order. It undercuts the overall impact and will likely annoy jurors in a couple of ways. In addition to having to cross a narrative gap to accommodate an out-of-order witness, jurors are also annoyed to hear that the availability of a witness is limited and has to be heard out of order. After all, they've had to make sacrifices to serve on the jury, why can't the witnesses do the same? When you do have to shuffle the witness order, it's crucial that you provide the nonsequential testimony into the proper context.

Anyone reading a George R. R. Martin ("The Game of Thrones") novel will unexpectedly come to a chapter with pages of lineage that interrupts the main narrative. All you want is to know what happened to the dragons, and here are several pages of some ancient family tree. If you're like me, you're confused and irritated, and you skip the chapter to get back to the part of the story that interests you. The same thing happens on a jury.

When ordering your witnesses, remember, too, that every trial (like every story) has three parts: a beginning, middle, and end. Your witnesses should follow that same natural order, explaining what happened, what were the consequences, and what needs to be done as a result.

Another way to look at it is the three levels of curiosity most jurors experience. During voir dire, they have questions such as, "Who are you?" or "Who are they?" and you should have answers for them. During the opening statement, they'll wonder, "What's this about?" and you should supply the answer. As testimony begins, jurors think, "Okay, I see where you're going. But what is your proof?" This is what your witnesses must deliver.

During your opening statement, you established the narrative of the case, instructing the jury on what happened, why it is important, and what to do. You have persuaded the jurors to look at the case the way you do. But as testimony begins, jurors need a third party to confirm that narrative. This is where your first witness must stand and deliver. The first witness must affirm the story you told the jury in your opening, sketching outlines that subsequent witnesses will fill in with color and depth.

In effect, the first witness tells the jurors that, "Everything you just heard in the opening is true, and this is why." The jury wants that confirmation right away and expects it. The jury learned to trust you during voir dire, and the first witness convinces them that they can also believe you. A good start like this frees you up to emphasize damages and suggests to the jury how it can act to deliver justice and undo the harm done. Other subsequent witnesses may fill in the story with additional supportive evidence and nuances in the natural order of the story, but it is very unlikely that they will carry as much weight in testimony as that first witness.

Never put a damage witness on the stand first. It will undermine your credibility. Although all witnesses should reinforce damages, jurors must first be convinced of the righteousness of the cause. Presenting a damage witness right out of the gate can be viewed by jurors as manipulative, as an appeal to their emotions, and this will only feed into the pervasive bias against plaintiffs that their case is about money and not about justice. Although you should always look for opportunities to illuminate damages, even with primary liability and causation witnesses , you should not lose sight of the primary focus of their testimony.

In many cases, an expert witness should be your first witness. An expert will explain the evidence and help the jury to understand its importance. An expert can also provide a cognitive framework for the testimony to come and inoculate jurors against the wild hypotheticals that are likely forthcoming from the defense. They can teach the jury on the significance of the evidence and why so that their subsequent understanding of the evidence is understood the way you intend.

In other cases, the best first witness is an eyewitness who can definitively identify the defendant as guilty. In auto negligence cases, for instance, these witnesses provide irrefutable evidence of guilt while putting the jury on the scene in an unforgettably raw, pulse-quickening way. Once this first witness has brought the jury into that vivid moment, your accident reconstruction expert can take the stand to explain the science around what the eyewitness just described. This is a powerful combination. Be sure the lay witness is definitive. However; if they are undermined by an effective cross-examination, it will create problems for the rest of the trial.

In some cases, it can be more effective to have your expert first reconstruct the accident and explain the science. Once that foundation is set, it reinforces the credibility of subsequent lay witnesses who can describe in compelling terms the human toll of the event.

Once you have presented your best witnesses on liability and causation, alternate additional testimony on these issues with damage witnesses, gradually shifting focus exclusively to damages. Although this provides some flexibility with the scheduling of witnesses, try to keep to the story fluid and coherent. After the best non-damage witnesses, alternating liability witnesses with damage witnesses serves as a reminder that, "They did this."

Your final witnesses should be your best damage witnesses. A great story builds to a crescendo and the damage witnesses in a trial should do the same. The emotional impact of that witness will spill over into the defendant's case. A defendant following compelling emotional damage testimony with a sterile liability witness can be interpreted by jurors as being callous and an attempt to divert or deceive. Presenting economic damage experts last is usually a mistake because it can dilute the emotional impact of the damage witnesses and therefore provides a more conducive start to the defense. Non-economic damages are arguments, and those arguments are better received by jurors who are still responding to that last powerful testimony.

In most cases, the best damage witnesses are the client or family members. They can communicate the meaning of the damages emotionally as well as practically.

Some attorneys rely on recorded testimony from their experts. This is a mistake for several reasons. First, recorded testimony is always less persuasive than live testimony. Jurors find that being able to "look in the eyes" is more convincing than looking at the screen. Second, trials are dynamic and so pre-recorded testimony lacks the flexibility to emphasize evidence that subsequent testimony might undermine or makes even more persuasive. Some issues only emerge during trial that might require testimony from your expert that was not explored earlier. Sometimes expert witness schedules cannot be modified, but pre-recording testimony should be vigorously avoided.

Keep in mind that some clients can't communicate damages better than their loved ones. Clients with traumatic brain injuries can appear "normal" because the brain impairments don't emerge in normal conversation. They may also have anosognosia, or damage to their proprioceptive abilities, and they cannot recognize their own impairments and deny that they have any.

Have a neuropsychologist or psychiatric expert testify first to put the plaintiff's denials or inconsistencies into context. This testimony will help the jury understand inconsistencies in previous testimony and allow them to see it as confirmation of the damages identified by the expert. It's not dishonesty. It's damage. While an expert can put previous damage testimony in context and enhance the credibility of the testimony, the last few witnesses should be lay witnesses who provide the most emotional and meaningful damage testimony.

The final witness carries nearly as much responsibility as the first. The final witness instructs the jury on how to understand the testimony they've heard. They distill the damage proofs to meaning and define the outline of justice in the case. Your last witness makes it clear what the jury must now do.

To understand the disproportionate power that your first and last witness have, keep in mind an important psychological principle called "primacy and recency," which occurs when the first and last stimuli have disproportionate influence over memory and subsequent behavior. Thus, have your best witness on liability go first and your best witness on damages go last.

Key Takeaways
- Plaintiffs and witnesses struggle to discuss the damage they suffered because they've spent so much time and effort—emotionally and physically—to overcome their injuries. Acknowledging their pain and suffering and helping jurors understand them runs counter to all your client has been working towards. It feels like they are moving backward, and they will fight that unless you convince them to suspend the denial and minimization they've adopted to heal.
- Spend time getting to know your witnesses. If you can make them feel comfortable with you, they are more likely to participate in helping you create an effective narrative.
- Never coach a witness but help them understand what the case is about and how their testimony will fit in. They are confirming, not constructing, the story you tell in court. Reduce their anxiety about testifying by discussing the logistics of their appearance and what to expect when they take the stand.
- Help witnesses develop cogency and direct, specific testimony by asking them clear questions and reflecting back to them what you hear them testify to. Identify and understand their experience; this will help them open up and help them heal from their own suffering.

- Lean into testimony about the little details that reveal damages- the plaintiff who needs assistance after using the bathroom, the survivor who has yet to change his dead partner's pillowcase because it carries her scent. This is how jurors truly feel the pain endured; they can relate to it.
- Use expert witnesses who believe in your case and have an unwavering commitment to their opinion. They should use simple, understandable language. Take time to get to know them; understanding how an expert views their place in the world helps you phrase questions consistent with their defenses.
- Establish a logical order for your witnesses that follows the narrative of the story you've told. Scrambling the order or witnesses does little to reinforce the narrative you want the jury to adopt. Each witness should pick up where their predecessor left off and deliver timely answers to questions as they form in jurors' minds.

Chapter Six:
Understanding Damages

Mary Curry was driving with a friend when their car was rear-ended by a semi-truck. Mary and her passenger were both trapped in the crumpled vehicle as it began to burn. Some bystanders were able to pull Mary from the burning vehicle, but they were unable to free her friend from the wreckage and watched in horror as the flame engulfed her friend. Everyone nearby, including Mary, could smell her burning flesh.

Mary eventually sued the trucking company, and I worked with Geoffrey Fieger on the case. Although Mary's physical injuries included a four-inch gash to her head, her greatest injury came from Post-Traumatic Stress Disorder. Although most people associate PTSD with combat veterans- it used to be referred to as "shell shock" or "combat fatigue- the truth is that anyone who's been in a serious accident or threatened with violence or rape can develop the condition. It leaves them with intense, disturbing thoughts long after the accident has occurred.

They can have nightmares and flashbacks, and they suffer lingering and debilitating sadness, fear, or anger. They feel estranged from other people. A smell, a sound, a glimpse of something can trigger in them a sudden sensation that they are reliving their horrifying experience. Women are twice as likely to suffer from it as men. Even witnesses to a tragic event can develop PTSD and have it haunt them for the rest of their lives.

Before we asked Mary to take the stand, we provided the jury with exquisite detail on how Ms. Curry had experienced PTSD. A forensic psychiatrist testified to Mary's PTSD and educated the jury on the biology of PTSD, as well as its medical and psychiatric problems. He explained to the jury what to look for as evidence of the condition. As Mary testified, you could see jurors leaning in to hear her, and many were almost imperceptibly nodding as again and again they spotted signs of PTSD in her manner and the way she spoke. When Ms. Curry's therapist took the stand to confirm the diagnosis of her PTSD, many jurors were already convinced.

Although the jury returned a favorable verdict, the truth is that the trial itself had more value to Mary Curry than any amount of money. In the telling of her story and having the jury believe it and take up her cause, Mary was able to begin the healing process. Seeking and finding justice is healing work.

My point here is that an effective demonstration of damages is more than a vehicle to large verdicts. It is a vehicle for recovery. It has a profound palliative effect. As a psychologist, I see this more clearly than most lawyers, and I always implore plaintiff attorneys to keep this in mind as they present damages during a trial. The more thorough your presentation of damages, the more complete your client's healing will be. This perspective will help you understand the true value of developing a compelling display of damages.

Finding the Damages

Understanding the damage done to a person is always a matter of context. How that person experiences those damages, expresses the damage, and how you come to understand that damage to them is more than just the most important process of building the case—it is also a part of the healing process for every client. That healing process often starts when you become an advocate for your client and come to understand and appreciate the full extent of their pain and suffering. Your willingness to take a risk and to fight for the victim has a restorative effect that goes far beyond financial awards.

Consequently, consideration of damages should permeate every phase of the trial from preparations to closing. Follow the mantra: "damages, damages, damages." Ask yourself how any evidence might relate to damage. Make it a reflex: *Where are the damages in this evidence?* or *Does this witness have anything to say that might relate to damages?* All personal injury trials are about damages because it is in the reparation for damages that justice is done and lives are repaired.

Take the time to show every exhibit and get in every bit of damage evidence. Look for damage testimony from every witness, even the defense witnesses (damage testimony from a defense witness can be unexpected but has a tremendous impact). Provided the demonstration of damages is authentic and not redundant, you cannot overdo it. Being thorough and persistent establishes that the damages are real and meaningful. It establishes that you believe them and that you aren't exploiting the damage through excessive repetition or exaggeration.

If you're always listening for potential damage testimony, you can find it from witnesses focused on other issues. For example, an eyewitness describing the sights, sounds, and even the odors of an auto collision will often display signs of their own emotional trauma, providing valuable context to the power and violence of an accident. They think, "If the witnesses were shaken up and remained troubled by what they saw, imagine how the plaintiff suffered!" This increases the credibility of damage testimony later in the trial.

Overcoming Obstacles

Still, exploring damages in trials requires that you overcome some pretty significant obstacles. Witnesses and victims often resist talking about their trauma, and many attorneys and jurors are averse to it as well. Plaintiffs themselves may not understand their own damages and be incapable of fully describing how their lives have been affected. Their family members may be inclined to play down the damages suffered by a loved one. Jurors have a natural inclination to distance themselves from that trauma ("That never would have happened to me! I would have been more careful.") . This causes them to blame the victim for the accident they endured.

That's because emotions play a key role in the brain's reaction to the environment. We naturally try to dodge painful emotions; they are a threat we must avoid. If we can't avoid them, we try to deny or minimize them. Regardless of whether you're a juror, plaintiff's attorney, plaintiff, or a witness, your mind naturally resists testimony about pain, suffering, and disability.

Your job is to identify and over these obstacles. And you need to start with yourself.

Most attorneys would likely deny they have a problem, but your own emotional biases are the most common and significant obstacle and can hamper trial preparation and presentations. From an early age, we are all taught to "suffer in silence" or "get on with life" after a significant setback. We diminish our trauma in order to move past it. Reflecting on it is a sign that we haven't "moved on" and *this* is perceived as a weakness rather than the injuries we actually endured.

Whether they are willing to admit it or not, many attorneys feel this way and may subconsciously perceive their own client as a whiner or a malingerer who is exaggerating their pain. Whenever I hear an attorney label a client as a whiner, it tells me more about the attorney than the client. Our beliefs about how we should tolerate pain are almost always more intolerant of others than they are of ourselves. At an even higher level of irony (or hypocrisy, I suppose) is our belief that clients who have gotten back to a near-normal life- no matter how heroic their efforts were to achieve this- aren't as badly damaged as they claim.

As a plaintiff's attorney, you need to be willing to examine these biases or yours. The first step in getting past them is to acknowledge that they exist. You simply can't develop a compelling damage presentation if you're not recognizing your bias and actively tamping it down and developing authentic empathy for what your client has been through.

You may also have biases over gender or economic standing. In cases involving sexual exploitation, such as a teacher sexually abusing a student or a psychiatrist abusing a patient, we are less empathetic to male victims than female ones. Likewise, if a client is already rich, they may seem less entitled to damages than a plaintiff of poor or more-modest means. Rather than looking at what was taken from a victim, we look at what they have left, diminishing our perception of the damage that was done to our client.

These biases manifest in a lackluster effort to identify all elements of damage or dismiss entirely some elements of damages. You may not be aware you're doing this if you haven't taken the time for introspection to identify your biases. For example, traumatic brain injuries (TBI) are one of the most underdiagnosed injuries in medicine. TBI is rarely diagnosed by first responders and primary care treaters. Any force suffered by a person that causes damage to soft tissue is sufficient to cause a traumatic brain injury, yet medical records rarely document it. As the plaintiff's attorney, you must be aware of the possibility and actively rule it out if the injury has not been documented. If TBI is diagnosed, you must develop an understanding and appreciation for the long-term consequences of the injury. Only then are you prepared to present those damages to a jury.

This work on your part to overcome your biases continues through the trial. Attorneys often impose their own judgments on the "value" of damages by discounting some injuries or their client's career setbacks. ("They're getting around okay. They can still find work.") Then there are those who worry that they are harming the client or their case by fully exploring their client's pain and suffering so they prematurely cut short the testimony on it. Again, your inclination to think and act this way may be intrinsic, so you have to be conscious of this tendency and consciously work to overcome it.

Plaintiffs, jurors, and witnesses have their own biases to deal with. For many plaintiffs, their recovery requires that they actively avoid reliving their trauma. But trials require that they do this repeatedly, at a glacial pace. Acknowledge that fundamental contradiction. You are going to reopen old wounds, and your client may resist letting you do that. Help them understand what we talked about at the beginning of this chapter: that a full, honest, and authentic demonstration of their pain and suffering will not only help them achieve justice but it will help them heal, too.

By the same measure, many witnesses are trying to minimize their trauma and will want to avoid the emotional pain of recounting what they saw. In their minds, the less they remember, the less they say, the less they will have to relive how they felt.

Jurors, meanwhile, will have a much different reaction to damage testimony. When confronted with another person's trauma, they naturally try to relieve their anxiety by distancing themselves from it. ("Could that happen to me? No! I wouldn't let it! Why did this plaintiff let this happen to them?") Sometimes their reactions can translate to minimizing the damages to the client ("They can still walk, even if it is painful"). The distancing of people from the emotions associated with pain and suffering is a natural response. It can also trigger the same unhelpful emotional defenses in the jurors. This is why jurors who have had similar experiences are often the least favorable to select onto a jury.

Failing to Give Full Measure

There are a variety of reasons why attorneys fail to fully investigate all damages. Their biases may lead them to think certain damages are trivial or that PTSD is not worth the trouble or expense to demonstrate to a jury. In some cases, a client's pain and suffering rekindles unwanted emotions in the attorney or forces them to confront painful memories of their own. If your initial reaction to an injury is that it's "no big deal," you're posing a problem for your own case. You may be biased. All damages are contextual; they have to be understood in terms of the client's life, not yours or anyone who has not been similarly injured.

I've been involved in several trials that resulted in multimillion verdicts based on plaintiffs suffering from PTSD, but I'm amazed at how many attorneys won't spend money to work up evidence or testimony on that affliction. In truth, no damages to any human are too trivial to ignore. If we believe the damage was trivial, our presentation of damages will be trivial as well. Likewise, attorneys with an alcoholic patient often carry heavy emotion to cases involving that issue that diminish their effectiveness if they aren't aware of that bias and consciously work to overcome it.

Some attorneys find it too difficult to do a thorough investigation into how their clients must deal with a gruesome or disfiguring injury. Clients will be more sensitive to their attorney's avoidance of that disfigurement than they are of the disfigurement itself. They learn to live with the disfigurement, but the judgment or rejection of others to that disfigurement is much harder to accept or ignore, particularly when it's your own attorney. In these situations or in cases of race or gender, an emotionally astute attorney has an advantage. The first questions they ask are directed at themselves and explore what biases they have that might interfere with understanding the damages and the effects on the client.

These biases affect how you communicate damages to a jury but also how you coax the truth and depth of injuries from your client. You can't be seen judging what your client is telling you; victims are often hypersensitive to the judgments of others and will see your attempt to disguise it, just as the jury will at trial.

For example, I was asked by an attorney to assess the virtue of a case involving a veteran who was sexually exploited by his Veteran's Administration psychiatrist. The issue dealt with gender bias: the vet was a male and the therapist who raped him was a woman. The case had bounced around several law offices, with most of the attorneys turning it down while wondering out loud how they, too, could get an appointment with such a doctor.

But this was no joke. The vet had a history of multiple concussions from IEDs, suffered from PTSD and depression, and endured chronic pain from multiple orthopedic injuries. When he sought help at the local VA hospital, the psychiatrist offered "therapeutic massage," which led to several sexual encounters that worsened the veteran's depression and did untold damage to his marriage. The attorneys who initially considered the case felt the obstacles were too great to give the case any value.

Moreover, the veteran was psychologically tested and showed a marked tendency to exaggerate symptoms. He had specifically requested a female therapist.

As a child, he'd been sexually abused by a female babysitter. The deck was stacked against this "Devil Dog," and one attorney after another discarded the case with derision if not outright disdain. Of course, if the vet had been a woman and the therapist a man, their reaction likely would have been quite different. None of these attorneys would have a problem characterizing this as rape. But the victim was a Marine with extensive combat experience.

We took the case anyway. We saw the inherent gender bias and first worked to overcome our own biases before building a case for the veteran's pain and suffering. We made the case that the duty of a therapist is to never relax the therapeutic boundaries and we produced experts who testified that what had happened was clearly sexual abuse- rape. The veteran had never consented, and we were able to take adverse evidence, such as the psychological testing and the veteran's request for a woman therapist, and made it supportive. We were able to show that victims with chronic pain typically appear to be exaggerating symptoms on neuropsychological tests and that the veteran's request for a female therapist was normalized due to the fusion of nurturing and sexuality established in him through sexual abuse he suffered as a child. The context shifted drastically; this was not a war-hardened vet getting laid by his lovely psychiatrist but a vulnerable, injured victim being exploited in a twisted, unethical, and damaging psychological gambit by his predatory physician.

Another mistake attorneys make is in feeling they need to "rescue" a client in distress. When their client is sobbing on the stand, some attorneys will curtail their questions- either out of sympathy for their client's pain or out of guilt for the trauma they are asking them to relive. Some attorneys will back off out of fear they are alienating jurors by probing these open, gaping wounds.

However, backing off is a mistake. The pain must come forth. As the attorney, you don't have to relish these moments, but you can't withdraw out of pity either. One of the hardest skills I had to learn as a therapist was to allow the patient to feel that pain. I understood that the catharsis was necessary for both of us- for them to let go and for me to understand. The same is true in the courtroom. For the client to truly heal, they need their pain to be understood, appreciated, and validated by a jury of their peers.

A false sense of compassion could cause you to avoid exploring an injury out of concern that you are making the client feel self-conscious. But that false solicitude can cause the opposite problem as well. Sometimes a contrived empathy can cause an attorney to become sadistic and exploitative of the pain. Our own emotional reactions affect our work in presenting damages in subtle but significant ways in every trial. Again, the capacity for introspection and the emotional acuity of the attorney are tremendous advantages in overcoming these personal obstacles.

It's Worse Than You Thought

Your client's damages are almost always worse than what has been documented or identified. Attorneys make a huge and avoidable mistake when they fail to develop a complete understanding of the full extent of those damages. It's not enough to merely compile medical records. You must develop a technical understanding of how an injury or other type of damage occurs and is experienced by any human being and then apply that knowledge to your client. It's vital that you know how your client was affected but also how your client *could be affected in the future* from the injuries they sustained. You can't rely on witnesses or doctors for a full understanding.

Remember, too, that all damages are contextual. How, for instance, do these damages uniquely affect your client? What do these damages *mean* to them, not only to their health but also to their peace of mind and future aspirations? This is a vital piece of the meaning for your case, and you can't rely on easy answers or outsiders to fully deliver this crucial understanding.

When I was a therapist for professional sports teams, I learned what it meant for athletes to suffer career-ending injuries. Most didn't suffer financially, but the existential damages were devastating. For many, their sense of self and meaning was tied to competing and winning, and now they were being deprived of that. To appreciate what they endured, jurors would need to understand the context of how the athlete rose up and into their profession, and the sacrifices and the emptiness they felt when deprived of the status they worked so hard to achieve.

Medical records won't provide much context either. Medical reports describe the medical treatment and are written for other medical professionals, but they do little to describe what the injury means to the patient. What does it mean to your client to have a broken bone? How is a spiral fracture different from a compound fracture? You won't know until you explore the likely and potential consequences of damages.

For example, what is the difference between a broken tibia and a broken ankle in terms of pain and how your client will function? A broken ankle is more painful, significantly impairs walking and weight-bearing, and takes longer to heal. This injury is far more significant for someone who needs to move around for their job than for someone who sits at a computer terminal all day. But for both people, it can lead to significant back problems from gait maladaptation or crippling arthritis several years from now.

Understanding the damages means understanding the potential collateral damages or sequelae. Sexual abuse of a child affects their present physical and psychological state, but it will exert even more profound effects later in life on their personal and professional relationships. It affects future earning potential. Chronic pain often triggers major psychiatric illnesses in the future. A breach of contract can cause credit issues and future sales declines. Damages can alter the arc of a business or human life. Knowing the potential collateral and future effects of damages is a key part of developing damages for trial.

Don't count on your clients to provide the full picture you need. They may have emotional resistance to acknowledging their impairments. They may fail to attribute some problems to their initial injury. For example, one symptom of a traumatic brain injury is agnosia. The area of the brain that regulates proprioceptive cues is impaired and the person feels perfectly normal even with significant impairments. They may feel comfortable driving even when their vision is severely restricted. Again, understand that humans have an incredible capacity to deny pain or discomfort to function in daily life. They are trying every day to get past their trauma and compromised facilities, and you are asking them to pause that process and explore the full damage they've endured. It's for the good of their fight for justice, but it creates an internal struggle, a fight in their mind of opposing forces. To help them in this battle, you must respect their defenses and adaptations.

The truth is, no one is better suited to look at the comprehensive picture than you are: the doctor won't, the client isn't capable, and the defense certainly isn't going to help. It's up to you to find the potential ramifications of your client's injuries. This is why some of the best personal injury attorneys often sound like they also have a medical degree; they are not intimidated by medical lingo and know what kind of questions to ask doctors to bring out the full extent of a person's injuries.

The Full Extent of Damages

A great way to identify the extent of your client's damages is to spend time with them watching how they live. In one case, our client was an elderly woman injured in a collision. The biggest loss in her life, she said, was no longer being able to compete in a golf league she helped start. Since most jurors would not relate to that, we spent time with her at home and learned just how much her life had been compromised by her injuries. She couldn't reach for a glass of water without calculating whether the pain involved was worth the reward. When she used the restroom, she needed help cleaning herself. These intimate, humiliating details which did not come up in our conversations with her were crucial in helping the jury understand how much damage our proud, independent client suffered in the collision.

We can use phrases like "pain every day, all day long," but the true impact is in the details, the specific examples of how your client can no longer take for granted things the rest of us do without thinking. Clients often adapt to their pain and suffering so these little things are often obscured to them.

One way to get at these obscure damages is to ask yourself how *you* might be affected by the same injury. Ask yourself, *How would this affect my life and my sense of self?* This kind of reflection will lead to insights but also to questions that will prompt your client to volunteer effects or consequences they otherwise may have not volunteered. Perhaps they thought it was too insignificant to mention. But it is in the mundane minutiae of everyday life that the relentless and uncompromising effects of an injury emerge.

You must overcome your own fears to thoroughly understand the injury and its effects on your client's life. Don't be afraid to look at the injury and ask questions. You don't have to hide your reaction to disfiguring injuries; most injured people are less afraid of your reaction to the damage than they are of being rejected or abandoned after the reaction. If you avert their eyes or avoid looking directly at them, they perceive it as rejection. So it's vital that you express your feelings while continuing to support their emotions and admire their adaptations to it. You want to communicate acceptance as well as understanding because that is very healing for the clients. They know that you've seen them and still want to work with them and advocate for them. In this way, you help them overcome their isolation, alienation, and hopelessness so they can get better.

Here again, authenticity is imperative. To uncover damages that the client is reluctant to reveal, you must have a discussion, not an interview or an examination. You have to overcome your own disinclinations and biases. If you've done sufficient introspection and have developed compassion, the client will trust that you appreciate the damage and pain they've suffered. However, you can only encourage them to discuss what they've tried so hard to suppress if they feel they can trust you not to push them too far. It may require several conversations before this trust and insight develops

How do you know when to probe and when to back off? It's something that you have to learn about each client, and you must learn it before they take the stand. You can pick up nonverbal cues that it's time to back off, decompress, and perhaps return to the topic later, much like you move a microscope lens back and forth while bringing your subject into sharp focus. This blurring and sharpening is valuable learning for you that will pay off when you talk with them about damages during the trial. You are learning just how to get the damage testimony out of the client in a respectful, caring way.

Remember, compassion is not a technique or a skill. Compassion comes from true understanding and respect, and if jurors see this in you, your client's testimony will resonate deeply with them. At the same time, an attorney who plunges into these sensitive areas with cold calculation and exploitive intent will be punished by the jury as a sadist. Understanding and empathy are important qualities that make it more likely that you will elicit compelling damage testimony and do it in a way that does not alienate a jury. Without that authenticity, your interest can be felt as a morbid curiosity rather than compassion.

As a psychotherapist, I learned that therapy is painful to the patient, often acutely and immediately painful. For the patient, therapy is like a broken leg that did not heal properly and needed to be rebroken and reset before it was whole again. So it is with their psyche, and so it is in trials. Trials are like going through the pain of refracturing the original injury and setting it right so the patient can fully heal. That is often how a client experiences the trial, especially the damages presentation: opening old wounds. Trials are emotionally draining for the attorney, but they are painful for the client. It's hard on them, and if you fail to understand this, you will fail to present a good damage case during trial. Being compassionate or at least considerate of their pain when discussing their damages is essential to get all the evidence you need at trial.

Money: The Big Obstacle

In addition to understanding the damages, the context, and the significance of damages to a client another huge obstacle to effective damages presentations is the bias against monetizing damages as a measure of justice. Money amounts are one of the most delicate and difficult issues for attorneys in any civil trial, and when and how to discuss this issue with jurors depends on timing and preparation.

While you can address this bias in voir dire, you should wait until closing to discuss money amounts. You can't overcome jurors' bias against money until they understand and appreciate the damages. They must believe the damages are real, significant, and unjustly inflicted before they hear a specific money amount to consider to deliver justice.

The issue of money is the elephant in the room. This is the only way jurors can mete out justice, but the idea of compensating someone for things that can never be replaced or healed is a foreign concept to most people. Some even find the idea distasteful, so it requires time in closings to help jurors understand why they are being asked to provide justice in this fashion. The only way to bring them around to the idea is when they have a full appreciation for how the plaintiff has suffered.

First, never use the word "award." Awards are something a person gets as a gift or earns for their performance. This connotation makes it even harder for jurors to accept it as a form of justice. How is being damaged an achievement, unless the suggestion is that the victim worked hard to be victimized? How is a victim "awarded" for having the priceless stolen from them? How is damage such as chronic pain and disability an achievement?

When an attorney talks of compensation as an award, they communicate a distortion of justice, which is not the effect you're looking for. Be mindful of the words you choose when explaining compensation for damages. Which words have more effect on you: to say that a client has been "denied" the loss of the companionship of their spouse or had it "stolen" from them? Certainly, those words carry a stronger connotation than "award," which suggests you are asking jurors to "give" money that is not theirs.

It's easier for jurors to understand money compensation as a symbol of justice. They are compensating for categories of physical and emotional damages, such as pain, disfigurement, humiliation, embarrassment, and so forth, but since some things, like the loss of life, are simply not compensable for any price, the money must serve as a symbol. "Just compensation" conveys the importance of what the plaintiff lost and what the defendant took from them. Will it make things right? Of course not. But to do nothing, to provide no compensation or token, minimal compensation only compounds the injustice your client has endured. This is the jury's only way to restore some semblance of balance, some acknowledgment of how your client suffered.

Explain the distinction between compensation for things like conscious pain and suffering that was unjustly inflicted and the pain and suffering that we all experience in life without compensation.

Jurors often think, "Well, I had pain when I broke my leg, and no one gave me money," or similar thoughts. We could all say that, of course, but how many of us could say that our pain and suffering had been unjustly inflicted? If it had been, wouldn't we have sought some recognition of that injustice? For the person not injured or damaged, money is just money. For the victim suffering intractable pain or who has suffered irreplaceable loss, money means something very different. Help the jurors to understand that it is not just the pain but how that pain was inflicted that is the issue. The act that inflicted this unjust and undeserved pain and suffering distinguishes it from ordinary pain and suffering and justifies compensation. After all, we compensate disabled veterans. We compensate victims of crime.

This idea of compensation as justice empowers your champions on the jury. They understand and appreciate the extent of the damage. They understand your client's pain and suffering. They've recalibrated their understanding of what compensation means in the courtroom and the trial. It's not an award. It's not a gift they are doling out. It's a gesture, an acknowledgment that a wrong was committed and that justice is required. It will not make the wronged whole but perhaps it will help them heal.

In Mary Curry's case, which I described at the top of the chapter, the jury felt her pain and suffering. When the damages expert for the defendant trucking company took the stand, the jury had already concluded that the plaintiff suffered from disabling PTSD. The expert psychiatrist had the unusual experience of being at Khe Sahn during the brutal siege in Vietnam near the Tet Offensive. We correctly inferred that he had been traumatized himself by that experience, so we encouraged him to talk about the lasting trauma he had witnessed. Finally, he began to talk about the enduring effects on his own life.

Geoff Fieger, the plaintiff's attorney, deftly turned the defense witness into *our* expert witness, getting him to admit that Mary, in fact, had PTSD. Geoff focused his questions on the doctor's experience in treating veterans and crime victims with PTSD, bringing out the intractable severity of the impairments and unpredictable course the illness typically takes. The doctor even testified how combat veterans who had been in close proximity to burning bodies had the smell so indelibly ingrained in their senses that even decades later they would react violently to the smell of barbecued meat. Jurors couldn't help but recall Mary's testimony about seeing and smelling her own friend burn to death while she watched helplessly. It was a subtle shift from testifying that Mary Currey was fine to manifesting how she could not be fine.

After that, the defense witness's efforts to minimize Ms. Curry's PTSD felt cruel. Fieger had done the careful work with Mary Curry to unearth the damages she was trying so hard to suppress and had conveyed proof of those damages to the jury. He hadn't settled for routine medical reports but had discovered unrecognized damages, patiently asking questions that allowed the plaintiff to reveal them. In the end, because we had provided the education needed to overcome biases and had provided compelling testimony about the long-term devastating effects of PTSD, the jurors felt our client's profound suffering and were compelled to provide justice. The result was a thirty million dollar verdict.

Key Takeaways
- Effectively establishing your client's damages can have a profound palliative effect. The more thorough your presentation of damages, the more complete your client's healing will be. Just your willingness to take up their cause has a restorative effect.
- Context, context, context. Understanding the client is the beginning of understanding their damages.
- Be persistent and thorough, though not repetitive, in presenting damages. This will help the jury appreciate the extent of the injuries.
- Presenting damages effectively is not easy; plaintiffs often don't understand the full extent of their injuries and their family members often want to downplay them. And jurors have a natural inclination to distance themselves from trauma and blame the victim. You, as the attorney, may have to overcome your own biases through careful introspection.
- Develop a technical understanding of how an injury or other damage is experienced and manifested, but also what the future effects of their trauma may be. You need more than dry medical records that do little to describe what the injury means to the plaintiff. No one- not the client, doctor, or fam-

ily member- is in a better position to see the comprehensive effect of damages than you are. Ask yourself, *How would this affect my life and my sense of self?* This may lead to insights but also to questions for your client that surface fresh information.
- When introducing compensation, never apologize for the amount you seek and never use the word "award." The compensation you seek is a symbol of justice, not a gift or a reward.

***

Exhibits in Personal Injury Cases

In general, I advise using a light hand when it comes to demonstratives in a personal injury case. Gruesome photos have a shock value, but the more that photo is shown, the more jurors adjust emotionally to it and the less impact it has in their final judgment. Some jurors are offended by graphic images and having clients display scars of other disfigurements can have a "dog and pony show" aspect that humiliates the client and offends jurors.

Often, the juror's imagination of the injuries being described will remain more vivid in their minds and have more impact than a poster-sized photograph that sits on an easel in the courtroom for an entire day. Still, photos of disfigurements or displaying disfigurements can be effective if delivered properly. They should be carefully revealed, *with the permission of the client in front of the jury.* Keep in mind that clients are much better at describing the disfigurement than medical professionals because the client can also put the meaning of the disfigurement into an emotional context.

There is a place for exhibits and demonstratives in some cases, such as financial disputes, but it's wise to keep them simple unless complexity is a key aspect of the damage. Organizational charts, cause and effect charts, and other visual means of simplifying and illustrating the testimony are more often helpful in these types of technical or complex cases, provided they help clarify the story.

Timelines can also be helpful in cases where chronology is vital to the jury's understanding. Timelines can reveal when interventions were crucial (or crucially missed), but many attorneys feel the need to complicate their timeline with extraneous information they hope will fortify their case. Fight that urge. Simplify. Timeline entries should be clean, straightforward, and linear, leading the jurors to the core conclusion (or damage) in your case. You can't bludgeon jurors with detail in an effort to show just how devastating your client's damages are.

Sometimes demonstratives are useful yet are utterly humiliating to your client. Balance compassion with your tactical considerations. If an exhibit is going to embarrass your client or traumatize their family—in full view of the jury—you can come across as sadistic and insensitive. In those situations, having your client and their family leave the courtroom can protect you from appearing insensitive *and* heighten the impact of your exhibit. It can foster a protective instinct in the jury, a sense that they have a role in nurturing your client back to health.

***

Examples of Often Neglected Damages

Researching damages involves more than gathering evidence from medical records and reports. It means understanding the implications of suffering the damages, identifying their distinct features, understanding how they are experienced, and learning how they are affecting your client. Here three of the most commonly overlooked damages in personal injury cases and how a little diligence can help you to identify and communicate damages more thoroughly.

1. Chronic Pain Disorder- This is one of the more overlooked damages in personal injury cases. Chronic Pain Disorder (CPD) is a brain injury stemming from chronic pain, often from spinal injuries. Patients who endure nearly constant pain for more than three months will experience changes in brain structure and function separate and distinct from the injury producing the chronic pain. The brain recalibrates its threshold for experiencing pain such that sensory stimuli not ordinarily associated with pain become interpreted as pain.

Physicians specializing in pain treatment assume the condition will develop in certain patients and don't always document it in medical records. You will have to ask the physician directly about CPD, and you should assume the disorder is present if your client has had chronic pain for longer than three months.

When someone has CPD, their pain threshold is lowered, making them more responsive to pain sensations that would not ordinarily evoke a response. Pain related to a specific injury evolves to where many experiences not directly related to the initial injury can cause pain. Clients with CPD live in a world of pain.

To make matters worse, a CPD sufferer's increasing complaints are often in-

terpreted as faking. During neuropsychological testing, the patient endorses so many diverse somatic complaints that the resulting validity scales often suggest they are exaggerating their pain. However, the pain they report is very real, and their CPD makes treating the pain from their initial injury less effective and more complicated. Their prognosis worsens.

CPD is often associated with the development of Major Depressive Disorder. The patient's chronic pain wears them down psychologically; they lose functionality and their suffering can be debilitating. Moreover, they lose hope and abandon the idea that the pain will someday end. This is why CPD patients often develop depression and suicidality.

If your client has CPD, you must communicate to the jury just how profoundly the pain has changed the plaintiff's life. When we say a client experiences pain most of the day every day, that vague and declaratory statement must be fortified with concrete examples of simple, daily activities that most jurors take for granted but are too painful for your client to perform. For the client who develops CPD, pain is not only a part of doing things, pain can also be caused by simply existing. That is an awful way to live.

2. Traumatic Brain Injuries - TBI is routinely underdiagnosed and unappreciated by first responders and treating physicians. Like Chronic Pain Disorder, it must be ruled out rather than ruled in. Any person who experiences enough force to cause soft tissue damage can sustain brain damage. It's often undiagnosed because:

First responders conduct triage and prioritize life-threatening injuries. If the patient is not unconscious or exhibiting signs of injury sufficient to score on the Glasgow Coma Scale, then the first responder looks no further. The Glasgow Coma Scale is used to identify potentially life-threatening brain injuries and not any brain injury.

Emergency Department physicians rarely test for brain injuries unless a loss of consciousness is experienced or reported. Many patients who experience altered consciousness rarely remember it or report it.

Radiographic tests such as CT, MRI or EEG rarely identify anything but the most significant brain damage, such as midline shifts initially or substantial volume loss post-injury. But TBI can still significantly impair brain function. TBI often isn't recognized by physicians, family members, and the patient. But their temperament changes, short-term memory problems, or heightened impulsivity nevertheless signal a problem.

The only definitive way to identify brain damage is neuropsychological testing, which can be expensive and is rarely recommended by treating physicians. In the military, soldiers who suffer a significant force during combat are automatically relieved of duties for several days and evaluated for TBI, regardless of their symptoms. Similarly, if your client has been involved in an auto accident and suffered soft tissue damage, you should also rule out TBI. Learn what to look for and ask the client and their family a lot of questions. Behavioral anomalies—preoccupation, forgetfulness, irritability—may signal TBI. The more symptoms you discover, the more likely it is that your client has TBI and the more compelling a referral for neuropsychological evaluation becomes.

Neuropsychological evaluation (not neurological evaluation) is relatively inexpensive. If the neuropsychologist recommends neuropsychological testing (a more expensive process) then it is worth the expense. Neurological exams are not the same as neuropsychological exams, and neurologists are not the preferred professionals for recognizing a TBI.

Neuropsychological testing is the gold standard for diagnosing brain impairments because of its ability to identify impairments to functioning. However, it can be difficult to explain to juries how impairment will affect your client's daily life. Your expert will need to translate those results into functional examples of daily living and any potential economic implications.

Neuropsychological testing incorporates validity measures to expose fake or exaggerated problems, thus providing objective. The defense bar has enlisted neuropsychologists willing to challenge the veracity of these tests, but the results they flag as invalid—such as an elevated score that suggests fakery—are often a sign of CPD. Ask your expert to explain results in terms of validity and how they translate to daily functioning. Neuropsychological testing is also useful in proving PTSD (where symptoms are episodic, unrecognized, or misdiagnosed) and CPD, which can appear to be malingering or exaggerating to the uninformed.

A TBI diagnosis proves present functioning impairments but also the likelihood of increasing future impairments. Damaged brains age much faster than undamaged brains, so you could argue minor impairments today are likely to worsen over time.

3. Post-Traumatic Stress Disorder- Any trauma perceived by the victim as life-threatening could cause PTSD, which triggers permanent changes in brain functioning and structure. For example, the brain's adrenergic receptors become denser and more responsive, increasing responses to stimuli. PTSD alone can be debilitating, but it can also foster substance abuse disorders, depression, and anxiety disorders. Patients avoid situations even remotely similar to their initial trauma, and they avoid talking about the trauma. They can seem reluctant to engage in the treatment, but their reluctance is actually a symptom.

PTSD is permanent, but the symptoms can wax and wane over a lifetime. The symptoms may not appear for weeks or months after a trauma. They may abate for years and suddenly and unexpectedly reappear. The only treatment goal is to control the severity of symptoms with medications or psychotherapy or both. PTSD can not only cause the development of other psychiatric illnesses but also can have adverse somatic consequences such as cardiac conditions. Psychological testing can confirm PTSD objectively.

Jurors accept the reality of PTSD as a disabling injury, but many attorneys discount the "value" of the injury. They have a bias or simply don't understand the severity of the condition. They associate PTSD with extraordinary combat trauma and not sexual abuse or an auto collision. They fail to learn enough to understand PTSD is a brain injury causing disabling symptoms.

***

Chapter Seven:
Closing Arguments

Your closing argument is the moment when you invite the jury to enter the narrative and complete the story you've started. As you summarize the evidence and the trial itself, jurors should feel their important role emerging; they've been passive listeners so far, but now their obligation, their responsibility, is clear and immediate. They understand the central conflict, they see who the victims and offenders are, and now they must decide how all the lingering questions must be answered.

Understand that jurors *want* to be inspired. They *want* to be involved in something important. No matter how reluctant they may have been when first selected, they are fully invested in this story now and eager to play their part. You must tap into that energy by inspiring and empowering them. It is time for them to deliver justice.

Finding Your Tone

Your tone in closing should reflect your authentic feelings about the damages your client has suffered. Some attorneys tap into their compassion for their clients to encourage jurors to help them put the victim's life back on track. *They've suffered enough. We will never make them whole, but we can try to make things right and just.* Other attorneys chose to tap into their anger and frustration at the defense's red herrings, obfuscation, and smoke screens and invite jurors to help send the message that deceit will not win the day. *Their indifference to her suffering is cruel. It's irresponsible. Let's send a message that they must change.* Whatever motivates *you* after all the months and years of work is likely the best pool of emotion to use to inspire and motivate the jurors, though your sense of what will best motivate jurors is a consideration to make.

Whatever tone you choose, focusing on your motivation to get justice for your client is better than letting your anxiety over the verdict dictate your closing's tone and content. Some attorneys allow their anxiety to convince them that everything rides on the closing. They have a false expectation that their closing will change the verdict. The truth is that jurors at this stage have already made their decision. Although some will change their verdict during deliberations, closings rarely change a juror's mind. What your closing *will* do, however, is reaffirm for them that their support for you is well-placed. They are fighting the good fight. Your closing should empower and motivate your champions to take up your cause during deliberations. Your closing must give your champions the ammunition they need in deliberation but also imbue them with a passion for justice on your behalf. You will be modeling that passion for them. The closing is your last best opportunity to affect the outcome.

Closing Structure and Process

Your closing should be thorough but you should not reiterate every piece of evidence. Instead:
- Make sure jurors understand the verdict form.
- Instruct and model deliberations on every verdict so your champions are prepared for those exchanges and have developed their arguments for opposing views.
- Summarize just the key evidence they will need to support the verdicts you seek.

Begin your closing by recounting the key evidence and key moments of the trial and then invite the jury to write the story's conclusion. Model the deliberations as you'd like them to unfold. Your goal should be to motivate the jury to write a conclusion in which the victim is compensated for what they've been forced to endure at the hands of the defendant.

Remember my mantra: damages, damages, damages. Although you can't assume the non-damage verdicts are sewn up and must concisely support them with strong evidence, the vast majority of your closing should focus on the damage evidence. Here are other strategies to keep in mind:
- Teach the jury the pertinent instructions using the verdict form. Use key evidence to illustrate the meaning of the verdict form and instructions, and

model the deliberations on that evidence. Present the strongest evidence in favor of the verdicts concisely, preferably in a list. A list forces you to be concise and reinforces learning. The goal is to provide your champions the tools to resist diversions, distractions, and distortion from adverse jurors.
- Don't assume your nondamaged verdicts are locked. Even if you feel confident in those verdicts, don't allow them to be a weak link in your overall case. When your damages case is particularly strong, defense jurors sometimes coalesce around weaker verdicts. Don't give them that opportunity. Fortify your champions with simple concise evidence for nondamaged verdicts. Remember, deliberations are a group dynamic; unpredictable issues can emerge, and resistant jurors (hopefully you have only one or two) will go to the obscure and irrelevant weeds to torpedo your case. All it takes is one piece of evidence to say "yes" to a verdict, and if you are fortunate then you might have two or three such clinchers.
- Keep it simple. Many attorneys, worried they'll miss a piece of evidence that might convince a wayward juror, cram their closing with too much evidence. This dilutes the effectiveness of your best evidence and gives dissenters ammunition to obfuscate or force attention on weak evidence at the expense of stronger evidence. Stay within the narrative you've constructed and deliver the evidence that most strongly supports it. When a champion can cut through a dissenter's diversions with a definitive statement of evidence that meets the criteria of the instruction, their opponent's patience to argue dissipates. When you model the deliberation on a verdict using concise examples and your best evidence, your champions will lead the jury to a quick verdict. The jurors want to do justice, but they also want to be done with it all and get back to their lives.
- Help jurors understand the proximate cause. The evidence does not have to prove that it is the only cause of damage, just that it is *a* cause of damages. This is about the only time you can discuss the burden of proof without suggesting an apology for the lack of evidence. Discussing the burden of proof earlier is a more difficult challenge than discussing it after arguing proximate cause. Then use the evidence to prove a cause as the only relevant cause needed for the verdict to be "yes."
- Take possession of the verdict form and instructions. Emphasize the criteria for verdicts and then use the evidence that clearly meets that definition as

an illustration of what that instruction means. In other words, coopt the instructions to increase the credibility of your evidence. You must own the instructions in terms of how they are to be used (and not misused) by the jurors and in terms of the evidence they define.

Three Tools: Form, Instructions, Evidence

Even though the judge in your case will give the jury instructions, it's a mistake not to reiterate and explain those instructions in your closing. Some attorneys ask the court to provide jurors with copies of the instructions so they don't have to rely strictly on what they heard.

As you review the definitions in the instructions, use the best example of your evidence on that verdict as an example of what the instruction defines. Here's an example of what you might say:

"The first question you must answer is whether there was negligence in this case. But what is negligence? Negligence is a failure to do something reasonable. For example, when the defendant failed to act on the symptoms of a spinal hematoma that were recorded in the medical record, it was unreasonable. Why? Well, you can use your common sense: if a life-threatening symptom is present, isn't it reasonable to expect the physician to address that symptom? Of course it is. Here is the evidence on the symptoms of the hematoma noted in the record Here is the evidence that the defendant ignored those symptoms. Here is the evidence that ignoring the obvious symptoms is a violation of the standard of care and that it was unreasonable to ignore the danger. ... That is what is meant by this instruction defining negligence, and this is how to fill out the verdict form on the question of negligence."

Here's another example from an auto negligence case:

This is the verdict form that you will be given. The first question you will answer is "Was the defendant negligent in one or more of the ways claimed by the plaintiff?" How do you know what negligence means or what evidence proves negligence? You will be guided by jury instructions that the judge will give to you. But let me help you get started. In this case, when the defendant failed to make sure the intersection was clear of other traffic, that was unreasonable and that means he was negligent. To prove he was negligent, we've offered several pieces of evidence, including the video footage from the traffic light in the intersection. That footage alone is enough to require that you write in "yes" on the verdict form.

When you provide a concise list of the strongest evidence, it serves as an example of what is meant by the instruction definition but also as evidence of the defendant's negligence. In closing, educate your champions on what each instruction means and how to use evidence to answer each question and reach a verdict.

One particularly effective technique is to use an enlargement of the verdict form and fill it out as your give your closing. This way, you model deliberations for jurors and thus speed up their deliberations. This helps prevent adverse jurors from misusing the instructions or otherwise complicating deliberations. The last thing you want is for jurors to struggle to reach verdicts on preliminary changes; when that happens, jurors are more likely to compromise later on money amounts for compensation. This almost always adversely affects the plaintiff.

Again, present your evidence as a concise printed list defining negligence rather than using the definition of negligence to categorize evidence. It should seem that the instructions were written for the evidence, making these two puzzle pieces fit together snugly. Your list will serve as an anchor that brings jurors back to specifics when their discussions lose focus. Give your champions the pithy proof to justify the verdict they're already reached and to deflect the dissenters' efforts to overcomplicate the case.

Some of the most successful trial attorneys I've worked with use flip charts during testimony. They write out summaries of key testimony and then return to those summaries during closing arguments. This brings jurors back to the key moment, rekindling the original impact of that testimony. The flip chart becomes a brilliant organizing tool for jurors.

As you reconstruct your narrative in the closing and invite jurors to write a just ending for the story, provide them a clear vision of what justice would look like from your perspective. If you have been authentic and if the jury trusts you, they will feel compelled to take up the cause and right a wrong.

Linking ALL evidence to damages

When discussing the evidence that defines negligence, point to the natural connection of negligence with the harm that was caused. For example, you might say: "This evidence is what is meant by negligence. We know that when someone does something unreasonable like this, it results in the kind of horrible damages my client suffered." In this way, damages can drive other verdicts.

Sometimes, damages can be so extensive that dissenting jurors will focus on other verdicts, such as negligence. For example, in the case of a baby who was horribly burned when a resident used a cauterizing pen in an oxygen tent, we were concerned that the one hundred million dollars economic damages compensation might compel dissenting jurors to challenge the negligence verdict. It seems obvious that using a cauterizing pen in an oxygen tent is negligent, but it was the only vulnerable target for adverse jurors to attack. Our closing put more emphasis than usual on negligence evidence, but we linked the negligence to the damage consequences to the baby. The resulting verdict was $128 million.

This does not mean you should use damages to justify other verdicts or vice versa. But it does mean linking the two. The persuasiveness of linking the evidence on those verdicts to damages is in the jurors linking in memory the actions or non-actions of the defendant to the consequences to the plaintiff emotionally as well as cognitively. Damages alone rarely ever are enough to gain a negligence verdict, but they can reinforce the effectiveness of the evidence on negligence.

Linking negligence evidence to damages can also be useful. When the defendant's actions are especially egregious, they can be considered damages by the jurors. This is particularly true in police misconduct or civil rights cases. For example, when an officer uses excessive force, that act in and of itself is damage, even if the force does not produce "excessive" physical damage.

In one job discrimination case I worked on with plaintiff attorney Jon Marko, an African-American woman with an impeccable record of nineteen years in the Michigan Corrections Department was transferred to an office where she was subjected to hostile racial comments and actions every day. On "Pizza Friday," her supervisor would single her out and ask if she wanted chitterlings on her pizza. The receptionist would frequently "slip up" and greet her with, "Good morning, mammy," instead of "Good morning, ma'am." A group of employees called her over one day to look at something they apparently thought was hilarious. They told her that a white parolee had adopted a "little black boy," and the irony was that the man's name was pronounced "coon." "Wasn't that hilarious?" they said. The Michigan Attorney General's defense was to suggest that Ms. Griffey had "misconstrued" comments as racist. After hours of emotionally exhausting testimony, the AG asked her, "Now Ms. Griffey, you know that comment wasn't meant to be racial, don't you? You know the family's name was spelled K-U-H-N, and that it had nothing to do with race?"

Marko focused on that incident in his closing, deftly attacking the AG's credibility by linking his legal defense to the acts of racism:

This was only one of the dozens of verbal assaults on her race. It was intentionally offensive. They knew it was offensive, she told them it was, and it was only one of the dozens of incidents that meet the jury instruction we discussed earlier and that the judge will give you shortly. But you also saw more than a little of what she suffered through and continues to suffer through even in this trial when the State Attorney defended that and other comments as "not racial"

Do you remember when she was on the stand? She had been testifying for nearly two hours about this and other verbal assaults and actions that actually endangered her life. She testified about how she tried every remedy possible, including formal complaints, but every complaint was dismissed, and retaliation followed. She was exhausted, struggling on the stand to maintain her dignity and not break down and cry after the two-hour-long litany of abuse that she had to relive. On cross-exam, the State Attorney asked her "Now Mrs. G., you know that comment wasn't racial in nature or directed at you, didn't you? You know that the name of the family was spelled K-U-H-N and had nothing to do with race, didn't you?"

What? Nothing to do with race because it was spelled differently from the identical word used to degrade African-Americans? This is part of what they do, and what they did to her for over a year. They're still doing it to her! The assault on who she was, the denials, and the further attacks of turning it around on her and trying to make her feel paranoid or foolish. The question from the attorney itself was offensive. Do you think that if someone had said "nigger" to her but spelled it "N-I G-E-R" she should not be offended? Or that it's about geography and not prejudice? That argument was not an appeal to fairness or common sense. It was an appeal to bias among you all. That's the defense—defend bias with an appeal to bias.

You saw how she reacted to his question, which was really more of an accusation. I could feel her reaction. How humiliating and embarrassing to have to face that in public in a courtroom, let alone every day at work. ... Look at this list: page after page after page of abuse... (Marko turned over each page of the flip chart for emphasis) These are only a fraction of the incidents that she complained about but was mocked or dismissed every time. You even saw it and felt it in the trial. These comments are what the jury instruction would define as ... The answer to the question on the form is "yes". This is the evidence, and this is how to fill out the verdict form with your verdict.

Nothing to do with race? Well, you will have a chance to say something about that with your verdict, because it should be clear by now that only your verdict, loud and clear, will put a stop to this painful mockery and humiliation.

Marko used the verdict form and instruction to categorize the evidence, and then he used the evidence to illustrate the definitions in the instructions. He had his flip chart with pages of comments with the names and dates of the testimony or exhibits. He had a blow-up of the instruction and the verdict form and went from form to evidence, evidence to form. He picked the right evidence to focus on and drew the jury into the story of the trial and then linked it to damages. The verdict of a jury of seven Caucasians and one African-American was unanimous, and the damages exceeded eleven million dollars.

By the same token, never miss an opportunity to link liability and causation to the damage aspects of the experience. Damages, damages, damages ... everything should ultimately point to damages. The initial stages of the closing are out of necessity more didactic, but once the verdict form and instructions are linked to a concise presentation of supporting the other verdicts, then the story-telling resumes with the arguments on damages.

Your Emotions and Demeanor

By the time you reach closing arguments in a trial, you're exhausted. You may feel anxious and filled with second thoughts. You might be excited, agitated, discouraged, or doubtful. Whatever your emotions, the jury will see them and might share them. Being authentic is important, but you must be aware of problematic emotions that might divert from your message. You have asked the jury to trust you and now you have to trust them.

Depending on what you feel and why you may want to share those emotions with the jury so they aren't misinterpreted. But in most cases, simply being aware of those emotions will keep you focused on delivering a clear message free of unhelpful sentiments you may be struggling with. The worst thing you could do is contrive or fake an emotion you don't truly feel. The jurors have seen you react and respond the entire trial, and contriving outrage or sadness or any other emotion during closing will undermine your credibility and effectiveness

Some attorneys are comfortable coming out of the gate on fire with emotion. Others project calm confidence or prefer cold anger to a hot one. The most effective approach is to feel what you feel even as those feelings fade and others emerge in the course of your closing. There will be times when you feel angry or indignant and other times when you feel sad. This is natural. Let it happen. Here are some other things to keep in mind as you deliver your closing:

- Energize the jury. You want the jury to go into deliberations eager to work, motivated to do justice. The defense has just closed by denying the truth and responsibility or somehow diminishing the value or worth of the client and the damages done to them. It's only natural for your authentic indignation and anger to surface.
- Again, focus the passion on damages. This is the verdict that is most tentative, and this is your opportunity to discuss money amounts because it is easier to attack a money amount that depreciates the value of damages that jurors have a complete understanding of those damages and their significance to the client.
- Defend your client, not yourself. Overreacting to personal attacks from opposing counsel will hurt your credibility, perhaps even more than the attack itself. The attack on you is a calculated diversion, a manipulation by opposing counsel, so don't play into their hands. This doesn't mean you should not respond, only that you should respond to the attack on you as an attack on your client. Any anger you display during the rebuttal must be in defense of your client. If you defend the value and worth of your client, jurors will view it as a defense of them.
- Carefully choose your demonstratives. As we noted in the last chapter, some attorneys effectively use flip charts throughout the trial to record important testimony. Watching the attorney make notes reinforces the learning and memory of the jurors. When the flip chart is brought out again during the closing, the pages reanimate the jurors' memory of testimony they heard days or even weeks earlier. Demonstratives of the verdict form, instructions, and a concise list of evidence can also help. Otherwise, I recommend minimizing demonstratives at closing. Demonstratives and visuals should enhance the story and not tell or be the story.
- Remain authentic. The presentation of damages is meant to motivate and is naturally more emotional. It is also cathartic, and you should let it out, but only what is truly yours. Fake indignation, sadness, or other emotions will be recognized and punished by jurors. A sincere recounting of the damages helps communicate the scale and impact of the consequences to your client.

Dealing with Attacks and Interruptions

Sometimes, circumstances such as an adverse judge or an obnoxious defense attorney constantly interrupting you will severely hamper your closing arguments and you won't be able to craft the tone and message you want. It's in these situations that you'll have to trust the jury. This takes courage.

In one case, Ven Johnson represented the family of a man killed in Washington after a helicopter suspending him flew into high voltage wires and the man plunged to his death. Throughout the trial, the judge made Johnson's life miserable. She raised her own objections and sustained them herself. She randomly interrupted his exams, insisting his questions were "improper." She continually reminded the jury that Johnson was from "out of town" and that "we don't do those kinds of things in this state." She refused to allow the forensic pathologist to testify about conscious pain and suffering while the victim was falling and refused to allow any testimony from a forensic psychiatrist.

It was never clear why the judge was so antagonistic. It could be she was angry the case hadn't been settled before trial. It could be that her niece was on the defense team (something the jury was never told) or it could be that Ven Johnson reminded her of someone who had traumatized her in past. Who knows what triggered her behavior. All we knew was that her animus toward Ven was visceral and unrelenting. She made little effort to hide her disdain for him.

The judge's bias hit a crescendo during the closing. Johnson had just argued that the terror the man felt as he plunged over 200 feet to his death was an element of damage and was therefore compensable. When Johnson covered the instructions on damages and began to cite the fear the victim felt as he fell hundreds of feet to his death, the judge jumped up and shouted "That's outrageous! There is no evidence that he felt terror while he was falling, and you will not get away with that in this courtroom. The jury will disregard his comment and your closing is finished. I want the jury to leave for the jury room and we will talk about sanctions."

The jury was just as surprised and confused as we were. Those of us at the plaintiff's table expected Johnson to be cited for contempt or not allowed to finish the trial. I ducked out of the courtroom at one point to call Johnson's firm in Michigan to see about getting money for bail. Eventually, though, Johnson was allowed to finish his closing, but the judge severely restricted it.

Later, the trial team was commiserating about the effect of the judge on the jury when we reminded ourselves: we asked the jury to trust us and now it was time for us to trust the jury. Throughout the combative trial, Ven had remained respectful and polite to the judge when the jury was present (although fierce and fearless when arguing his motions to the judge when the jury was not present) and his resistance to responding to personal attacks had heightened his credibility with jurors. Ven had remained focused on his client and the jury seemed to appreciate that. They came to see the judge's bias and responded with a multimillion-dollar verdict, including a substantial amount for the conscious pain and suffering of the victim, including the "fright and shock" of his horrifying fall to the ground. The point here is that juries will support you if you don't react defensively and continually advocate for your client. Jurors are fair and perceptive, and they like underdogs.

How you respond to attacks or unfair tactics can also be an opportunity. For example, during the closing by Gerry Spence in one criminal trial I worked on, the government prosecutor interrupted Spence at least half a dozen times in the first few minutes of his closing. Gerry could hardly finish a sentence without another objection being lodged. Whether it was a tactic to interrupt the flow or to irritate Spence, it was definitely frustrating the jurors.

Spence sensed their frustration and began to exploit the tactic of the prosecutor. He would make a statement, pause, and then turn toward the prosecutor with a grin and his hand extended in an apparent invitation to object. When the prosecutor objected to the invitations for him to object, the jury burst out laughing. Spence could have become frustrated, irritated, or even angry at the interruptions. Instead, he turned the tactic to his advantage.

Inviting Jurors to Finish the Story

If opening statements are when you tell the story of the case, closing statements are when you tell the story of the trial. Closing is not only a summary of the evidence, it's also a summary of the jurors' experience and the point at which the jury becomes part of the story. It is the point when the jury takes the burden of justice (the bird) into their hands. What will they do with it?

They must write the ending to the story you started.

Closing reminds jurors of that story and invites them in as authors. Closings bring the plot to the moment of their inclusion and point them to the ending that is just. How do you invite the jury to write the ending? Explicitly, by pointing out how they have already become part of the story and by outlining justice in money amounts. Bring the jury and their experiences during the trial into the closing.

Summarize the experiences of the trial, the experiences you shared with them. Here's an example:

We've come to the moment when you all finally get the opportunity to have your say. You've heard from the attorneys and the witnesses, and you've seen the evidence. We've been through a lot in this trial and we're tired. There have been times when we shared frustration at witnesses who wouldn't answer questions, or frustrated by the attorneys who couldn't stop asking questions. We've been surprised by some evidence, perhaps bored by other evidence. We've felt the pain and sadness of those who suffered. Through all of this, some of you had something to say or wished you could say something. I suspect that as much as I wanted to ask you what you thought during the trial, you wanted to let me know what you think. There were times when I saw you react to the testimony and could see how hard it was for you to stay silent.

Now, you get to have your say, and what you say is the only thing that matters. Even more than that, you have an opportunity that very few people have in life—an opportunity to do justice ... to right a wrong... to make a real difference in the life of another by providing the consolation of justice. Years from now, you will look back at what you did here and feel proud. I promise you. You not only did your duty, but you also created justice.

Soon you will have an opportunity to say the only words that will mean something and to do something that means all there is to say—to give us your verdict. To finish that part of the story and right a wrong. What kind of story will your verdict be?

When we first met during voir dire and talked about this trial and during the opening statement, I made you some promises. I promised I would tell you the story of what happened to my client and provide proof of what happened. I have kept faith with my client and kept faith with you, and now it's time for you to finish that story. You will write the end of this story on your verdict form. There is no other opportunity for my client. This is their one and only chance to get justice. For three years I have carried the burden of getting justice for my client. That burden will soon shift to you. You can finish this. Write the ending that fits the story we've started. What does it mean for you to do justice in this case? What was proven and what needs to be done?

You are passing the torch, handing off the baton. This is an archetype, and it resonates with jurors as a narrative imperative. It dawns on jurors that they are on a hero's journey. There is a path they must follow. They have a job to do, something significant. As screenwriter Javier Grillo-Marxuach once noted, a great (story) "creates an irresistible narrative flow that propels a reader to an inevitable dramatic conclusion."

Empowering the jurors is also an important part of the narrative current. Remember that the brain craves meaning, and jurors will respond to calls to action when they see they can change society or alter the arc of a suffering person's life. Help them appreciate the weight of the role and the significance of what they have done and sacrificed to be on this journey with you. Their service links them to the noble and their verdict is needed to heal or protect. It is fulfilling the scriptural admonition to "maintain justice and to do what is right." *Isaiah 51:1* You already understand the meaning of the verdict in this case, so communicate that meaning to the jurors in the way you feel it.

"Listen to me, my people; hear me, my nation: The law will go out from me; my justice will become a light to the nations. My righteousness draws near speedily, my salvation is on the way, and my arm will bring justice to the nations. ... But my righteousness will last forever, my salvation through all generations." *Isaiah, 51*

Use key moments from the trial to recall testimony and the jurors' experience in those moments. It has been days or weeks since they have heard and experienced your case, and the defense case has just been presented. Remind jurors of the actual testimony and how it affected them. At the end of a trial, everyone is exhausted from the emotional highs and from the lows and the boredom and the interruptions. Making the jury part of the story of the trial means more than describing or summarizing the key moments in the trial as well as the key evidence. It also means helping the jurors to recall their experience of those moments.

Recreating a Trial Moment

In a med mal trial involving a carpenter named Sal, we asserted that our client was abandoned in a hospital's emergency department while suffering an acute heart attack. Doctors had ordered that his vital signs be checked every fifteen minutes, but Sal wasn't checked for more than two hours. As a result, blood pooled around his vital organs, requiring the amputation of a hand and foot due to inadequate blood supply.

The hospital claimed vitals were taken, just not recorded. They were too busy caring for the suffering carpenter and other patients that they didn't take the time to do paperwork. The record-keeping was irrelevant anyway because Sal was getting the care he needed, they insisted. Besides, the lack of circulation was their fault but the fault of the medication provided; the patient had an acute, idiosyncratic reaction to it. In short, it was the classic defense trifecta: I didn't do anything wrong, and if I did it then it doesn't matter, and anyway it wasn't me, it was the medicine.

Late in the trial, a nurse took the stand and testified that she had been taking notes that day on napkins so she could enter them into the medical records later after all her patients had been stabilized. In fact, she had "just found" the napkin that showed all of Sal's vital signs recorded on it! She'd even signed and dated and made time notations on the napkin, giving it what she thought would be an air of officiality. We didn't get a copy of these notes until after the trial started, which was a nasty surprise that violated discovery rules.

The emotions of the jury were visceral. Everybody knew the case hinged on this nurse's testimony and on the veracity of the napkin. Jurors who had been leaning in favor of the plaintiff were confused and disappointed. Jurors supporting the defendant leaned back, feeling justified and vindicated.

However, Geoffrey Fieger, the plaintiff's attorney, had spotted something others hadn't. The signature on the napkin. "Can you read the signature on the napkin?" he asked the nurse. She glanced down and read her own name. When she finished, Fieger went on. "I'm struck by the last name you signed with," he said. "Is that your maiden name?" "No," the nurse said, suddenly going pale. "It's my married name." "I see," Fieger said calmly. "But you weren't married at the time you cared for my client, were you? Isn't it true that you weren't married and didn't start using this married name until *two years* after you treated my client?"

"Yes," the nurse said, her voice barely a whisper. "So, let me see if I understand this. You allegedly 'found' this napkin just recently, just before testifying, in fact. You testified that these are the notes you kept of my client's vital signs. To verify that these notes are legitimate, you signed, dated, and time-noted the napkin. *But you signed using a name you wouldn't acquire for another two years.* How do you explain that?"

Of course, the nurse *couldn't* explain that, at least in any truthful way. This twist in testimony had more than the usual impact because of the sudden swing of emotions. Our confused supporters on the jury were jolted back to believing the hospital was responsible, and the dissenters on the jury felt the floor of their room collapse. The verdict was probably sealed at that moment. When the witness was confronted with her false note, I saw that many of the jurors were upset or angry. One woman simply looked at us and smiled as if to say, "You got them."

This was a key twist in the trial, and Fieger wisely used his closing to remind jurors how they felt at that moment.

When the nurse first produced that note, I was as surprised as anyone else. We were never told that the note existed, and it felt like the case was slipping away. I looked at you all and saw you also were surprised and confused.

I also remember when I looked at the note and first realized she had been lying all along, which is why I didn't object to evidence that was unfairly hidden from us. She had signed the note with her married name, but she had already testified earlier that her name changed after she was married years later.

Then I felt a liiiiiiiitle different. I was relieved, but also angry. I looked over to you all to see if you all had got it and I saw how you were reacting. I saw the same emotions. We all felt the same way. Surprised and angry. It's a rare moment in a trial when the attempt to deceive you becomes so clear and the truth is revealed so clearly through that lie. Isn't it almost always true that the people who betray us eventually betray themselves? I don't know what pressure she felt to lie to you or who may have pressured her. I only know that this won't stop until your verdict makes it stop.

(At this point, Fieger's tone changed from relief to rising indignation and anger over the attempt by the defendant to deceive them—the jurors).

They NEVER took Sal's vitals. They abandoned him to suffer. They left him there as the blood drained from his arms and legs. It meant not just the loss of his hand and leg, but also the loss of his profession as a carpenter, the loss of his life as he wanted it to be. The loss of being the father he wanted to be for his baby, Michael. They took a lot more than just a hand and a foot.

They knew it then and they've known it since. But instead of regret, they refuse to take responsibility. Instead of giving Sal the dignity of the truth, they put forth witnesses willing to lie and records that have been altered. They try to cheat him out of justice. Why do they think they believe they could lie to you all in the jury and get away with it? In addition to the pain and the losses he suffers, he has also had to suffer the indignity of the denials and the lies. ... This is what is meant in the instruction by "humiliation."

One thing we can be sure of, and one thing that you can change: they know that justice in this case is not measured by millions of dollars but by damages that demand tens of millions of dollars. We can't replace his hand and leg or erase the memory of the trauma or the phantom pain, but one suffering you can relieve, and the one thing you can restore with your verdict is the dignity he deserves of the truth. He deserves a verdict that forces them to take responsibility for what they did to him. Let's look at more of the evidence of the negligence and the attempt to cover up that negligence ...

In that portion of the closing, Fieger put the jury back into the key moment they shared emotionally and argued the damages through those shared emotions and experiences. The attempt to deceive became part of the damages. The jurors felt that deception themselves, just as our client had. The result was a twenty-eight million dollar verdict.

Overcoming Money Bias for Damages

Damages dominate closing because money verdicts are the most difficult for jurors. Jurors rarely go into deliberations with their minds made up about money amounts, particularly for noneconomic damages. We've already discussed the natural biases we all have toward monetizing intangible things we value most in life. We say that things like independence, self-determination, health, and family are invaluable- and they are. They are so invaluable that putting a monetary value on them generates emotional resistance.

If we can't purchase them at any price and we can't replace them, how can we turn around and put a monetary value on them? If jurors are given a money value during voir dire, they will spend most of the trial asking if the elements of damage being evidenced are worth the amount requested. However, if you have not suggested a level of monetary compensation, jurors will focus on the extent and significance of the damages during the trial, and at closing, they are more open to considering money values.

Closing is the only advantageous time to address the bias against assigning money values to noneconomic damages. By the time closing arguments start, jurors have a complete understanding of the damages. The pain and suffering are no longer hypothetical but real and witnessed by the jurors during the trial. We're asking the jurors to pivot. They have to go from thinking that financial compensation is contrary to our values to thinking that compensation reflects the value we place on fairness and justice.

The money won't replace what was lost but it will signal that a wrong was done and that the victim of that wrong suffered meaningful damage. Once you've helped jurors understand this, you must motivate them to make the emotional investment needed to fight for the cause they have come to believe in. Jurors are not being asked to put a price on the *loss* of love, companionship, or any other priceless aspects of life. They are being asked to put a price on *justice for the loss* of those invaluable things.

To help them understand their resistance, closings should involve an honest discussion about that resistance. For example, most jurors think, *Why would anyone give money to a dead person? What good does it do them?* They might attribute your money compensation request to greed or some other bad motive. Address it head-on. Money compensation is the only form of justice for someone killed unjustly. Explain that pain and suffering inflicted as the result of negligence requires monetary compensation while the pain and suffering we all experience in life does not. The money isn't replacing what was lost and can't be replaced, but it is an affirmation of our belief in fairness and justice. Money provides consolation and acknowledges that a wrong was done and the victim's damages were meaningful.

The victim is comforted by the only justice possible- money, the symbol of worth and of value- and any justice, even symbolic, consoles victims and strengthens society. The bias against money verdicts can only be countered by a gentle redirection to our values and our willingness to act on those values of fairness and justice. One way to accomplish this is by giving examples of similar gestures in society. Here's is a story attorney Gerry Kenney used in one closing:

A few years ago, President Clinton awarded Posthumous Medals of Honor to members of the 442nd Infantry. The Japanese-American heroes from WWII were unjustly denied their medals while they lived. Many of them had died in combat, nearly all the heroes had died waiting for that day and medal. Getting the medal they deserved after being denied the medal meant even more than just the recognition of their valor to these Japanese-American heroes. These men who fought valiantly for their country all came from camps where they had been detained unjustly by their country. Denied their constitutional rights by the same country they fought and died to defend, they were then denied the recognition of their existence as much as their contributions.

Why give medals to the deceased fifty-five years later? Why do we give any posthumous medal? If we look at it only as a gesture to dead men, then it does seem meaningless. What good does it do? That's the real question—what good is done? Justice is not a gesture. Justice rights a wrong, and even if it is symbolic, it is healing. The medals were a symbol that valued their sacrifice, a comfort to their living families and most of all it corrected an injustice. To not "award" the medals would have been to continue injustice and a glaring denial that we really do value the sacrifice of the heroic lives.

Similarly, what good does it do to compensate a victim for their own death? Jurors ask "What good will it do them?" or think "It will only go to their family anyway." Well, I assure you that does a lot of good. It confirms the value and worth of that human life and affirms our value that all life is precious. To compensate a person for their death with a money verdict is a symbol of justice, but it is a justice deserved. To give no monetary compensation is to continue the injustice. The verdict is given to the victim who is certainly there to get it legally even if you don't believe they are there in spirit. Justice is not a thing, it is an act that is measured by fair monetary compensation.

The verdict in that case was six million dollars, with one million dollars to the deceased plaintiff. Here's another example of how you can identify and label the bias against compensating a dead victim. Juries commonly think in terms of money and not justice, and this is a bias attorneys have to alert them to. This closing models the deliberation for favorable jurors, providing them with the comments they'll likely hear from dissenters and then what their response might be to those arguments. Giving voice to the bias and explaining why it is bias and how to respond to it gives your champions a compelling argument to use during deliberations.

You might be thinking, "What good does it do to give monetary compensation to a person who has died? What are they going to do with it? The money will just go to the family or to the lawyers." Another question to ask is, "Would it be right to do nothing when a person dies unjustly?"

I think your answer to that question is that no life is worthless. The loss of life is worth something. This life had value and taking that life was unjust. If the life had value and its loss was unjust, we have a responsibility to address that. We have a responsibility to deliver justice. That's why we're here. Money compensation is the only form of justice we have available to us. To do nothing to compensate is to compound the injustice.

If we think only in terms of money and not in terms of justice, we misunderstand our purpose for being here, for having this trial. If we think only in terms of money and not in terms of justice, we are not only perpetuating the injustice, we are increasing the injustice. We're making it worse! You might hear someone say "We've already given the family money" as justification for not compensating the person who suffered the most damage. If there were no family members, would it be just to give no compensation to the plaintiff for the loss of their life?

The law requires you to consider justice for everyone separate and distinct. Justice is not a limited commodity. If you give the deceased fair and just compensation, it does not diminish the amount of justice available for other victims. This is a verdict separate and distinct from the other verdicts and the plaintiff deserves that consideration. And the law the judge will give you requires this consideration.

They say that those who die unjustly never have peace until justice is done. Justice matters to the dead as well as to the living. In fact, failing to compensate a victim who died unjustly would be to victimize them a second time. It would be a rejection of the value of their life. To give nothing is to give a verdict that their life was worth nothing. Those are not our values and that is not justice. Whether you believe it or not, they will hear your verdict. Do justice and let them rest in peace.

Calculating Compensation

Attorney James Harrington represented a plaintiff who was arrested in a case of mistaken identity. The police went to the man's place of employment, and in full view of his coworkers, he arrested him. The man, a young African-American, protested his innocence and showed them his state identification. However, the arresting officers refused to believe the identification and interpreted his protests as resistance. They wrestled him to the office floor, pepper-sprayed him, cuffed him, and took him to lock-up. The booking officer took prints and photos and locked him in a holding cell.

After discovering that they had arrested the wrong person, the police held him for an additional forty-eight hours, transferring him to the county jail while they searched feverishly for a warrant or some other reason to justify why they arrested the man. They couldn't find anything. The man was held another twenty-four hours before being released, but the trouble didn't end there. The man lost his job and the respect and trust of his coworkers, and had difficulty finding another job after the incident. This is how Harrington addressed the issue of compensation:

I struggled with how to put a monetary value on the damage done to Mr. B. Not so much for the humiliation he suffered when arrested while at work in a very public way, for being physically assaulted and incapacitated with a chemical spray, or the loss of his job afterward as the result. Fright, shock, humiliation—these are things that he suffered unjustly, and he should be compensated. The issue I struggled with the most is how to put a monetary value on the constitutional rights that were taken from him—forced to spend three days in jail. It takes on a particular significance to Mr. B. because his father was nearly killed fighting for the right to vote in Alabama when he was a child.

It seems like it cheapens our rights and our freedom to attach a money value to those rights. But the truth is that those rights have tremendous value. Generations of Americans considered these rights so valuable that they sacrificed their lives in wars in foreign lands and in the streets of America to safeguard them for us.

I was talking about this with a close friend of mine who lost his leg in Fallujah, Iraq, battling Al Qaeda in 2004. He told me it was worth the price he paid. Those rights mean that much, to him and those he served with. Those rights are so valuable to them that they are willing to make the greatest sacrifice to protect them.

And those rights are even more meaningful to a young African-American man because for too long in our history the message men like him got was that they were not human beings and did not have "inalienable rights." His father fought in WWII and in segregated Alabama for those rights. How do we put a money value on his rights that doesn't cheapen the value of those sacrifices? If others considered the same right as being valuable enough to die for, how do we put a monetary value on them when it is denied to the living? Mr. B. didn't die, but the value of his life and rights were taken from him by force—unjustly taken by force.

Justice in this case is measured in part by your affirmation that these rights taken from him do have value. Is $10 million too much money to ask for something this valuable to him? Money is the only remedy the law allows in this kind of case. I struggled to come up with a suggestion for you that won't offend you or cheapen the value of those rights or cheat him out of justice. After talking with my veteran friend, I learned that the death benefits for someone killed in combat is $500,000. It seemed to me that $500,000 for every day Mr. B. was falsely imprisoned and denied his rights is fair, reasonable, and just.

The jury doubled the amount suggested by Harrington and returned a verdict of three million dollars.

Comparative Fault

Another bias you may have to confront and identify in your closing concerns comparative fault, the doctrine in torts in which the fault attributable to each party is compared and any award to the plaintiff is reduced in proportion to the plaintiff's share of the fault. Juries lean into comparative fault reasoning because of our natural inclination to avoid seeing or feeling trauma. Our natural psychological reaction is to deny, minimize, or otherwise distance ourselves emotionally from that suffering, and one way to do that is to assign inordinate blame for an accident to the victim of the accident. Our brain wants predictability and control, so we naturally think about what we would have done to avoid the trauma. Processing a sudden, unexpected trauma or catastrophic injury challenges that sense of control over our lives, and the natural response of most people is to look for what can distinguish ourselves from the event.

We naturally drift to thinking about what actions we would have taken to avoid the same outcome- anything that can reassure us that it could not happen to us or a loved one. This natural tendency should be addressed in closing before discussing the evidence. To restore the jurors' sense of control and predictability, emphasize following rules and encouraging the jury to do what is reasonable. Control comes from predictability, so your emphasis is on the predictability of harm if rules are violated, and that negligence causes harm.

Jeffrey Stewart, a wonderful man and brilliant attorney, had a case of a client who rear-ended a stalled truck on a busy highway and died as a result. The defense argued comparative fault because, unlike other drivers, the client failed to stop or avoid the truck. During voir dire, Stewart was especially attentive to this bias, and in closing, he reminded jurors of their discussion as he emphasized the egregious negligence of the trucking company and the extraordinary effort and reflexes his client would have needed to avoid the collision. The result was a multi-million dollar verdict with no comparative fault attributed to his client.

When confronting comparative fault bias, appeal to the jurors' common sense and experience. The instructions that emphasize "reasonable" are themselves a call for jurors to use common sense. For instance, was it reasonable to expect Stewart's client to have the superhuman instincts and reflexes needed to avoid a high-speed collision with that truck? No.

In trials involving highly technical evidence, including med-mal cases, appeal to the jurors' common sense. Present evidence in such a way that the question,

"Does that make sense to you?" becomes a *coup de grace*. Still, common sense can be a double-edged sword. Sometimes common sense can cause us to overlook evidence to the contrary.

For example, standing in the middle of a flat desert under a blazing sun, our vision can convince us there is a shimmering lake off in the distance. But if there is a scientist in your caravan, she can quickly provide evidence to the contrary: the lake you're seeing is actually light passing through two layers of air with different temperatures, and the collision of air masses acts as a mirror. Even when we understand the logic behind the mirage, our brain struggles to override the emotional misperception that in just a matter of minutes you'll be diving into a cool, refreshing desert lake.

Here's another example: One of my hobbies is studying physics, and to this day, I dispute Werner Spitz, a world-renowned forensic pathologist who was a lead pathologist in the Congressional review of the Kennedy assassination. I argue that there was no way one bullet could enter JFK, exit him, change direction, and re-enter John Connolly. It defies common sense. Even though I understand that it is theoretically possible, my "common sense" and experience pull me to the wrong conclusion. (Or maybe I *am* right; Werner, are you ready to admit the truth?)

As you can see, it takes effort to overcome the common sense that contradicts the evidence, so you must alert jurors and help them avoid this tendency. In terms of comparative fault, they have to be steered away from thinking about what *could* have been done into thinking about what is *reasonable* under the circumstances. Preempt biased arguments in deliberations by modeling the response. Here's an example from an auto negligence case:

When people get caught doing something wrong, they respond in one of three ways. Usually, they deny doing it. They say things like, "It wasn't me. Someone else did it." If they can't deny what they did, they deny responsibility and blame something or someone else. They say things like, "It wasn't my fault. It was their fault." The third response is to deny any harm. "No harm no foul." Well, you heard all of the three denials of responsibility from the defense in this trial.

The defendants have tried to deny their responsibility for causing the crash. They hope you will not find them to be negligent. If you do find them negligent, then they hope you will spread the blame. They have claimed that (the client) was negligent ... that he also caused the crash. They hope you will blame their victim because they know that their financial responsibility will be reduced by every percentage of blame they can divert. They hope you will compromise by spreading the blame.

Overcoming Blaming the Victim Bias

The best way to forestall the effects of this "blame the victim" bias is to use your closing to alert jurors to this tendency. Provide the warning as well as the remedy. For instance, you might say, "If you hear a fellow juror speculating that the plaintiff could have avoided the accident altogether, remind them of the evidence we've presented that refutes that claim and ask them to stop." In this example, the attorney used himself to identify the bias and clarify the instruction:

You see, there is a natural tendency we all share, a bias really, that makes us vulnerable to blaming the victim of a trauma like this. I'm no different. When I first heard what happened, I was mortified at the damage done to my client. I thought, "Oh my God, that's terrible! What if that had happened to me or one of my children?" Imagining the accident happening to us or a loved one leads us to consider what we would have done to avoid the accident, and this creates a bias—that the victim deserves some blame for this accident.

When we learn of the unexpected death of a person, we naturally think about our own families and maybe then we might make a call to the kids or to our parents to say we love them and make sure they are safe. It's a natural response we all share. I know I hugged my wife a little longer when I got home from the office the day I learned about what happened.

But as I considered how to present the story of what happened, something unexpected happened. I found myself thinking about what I would have done to avoid what happened. I knew the facts and saw the evidence. I knew the law and the instructions on the law that would guide the decisions a jury would make. Still, I became that Monday morning quarterback we talked about during voir dire. We say that life is full of the unexpected, but when the unexpected happens we tend to say we should have expected it.

We could come up with a list of things that could have been done to avoid this crash, including not leaving home that day or taking another route. I did what people normally do to avoid the fear that something like this could happen to me or my family—I thought of things I could have done to prevent this from happening to me. Of course, none of the things I thought of had ever occurred to me before I heard what happened to my client, so it's unreasonable to believe they would have made any difference in the moment. Maybe some of you have already had similar thoughts during the trial. It's a defense really, an emotional defense against the fear that it could happen to us or someone we love. It's a natural reaction, a very human reaction to a tragedy. We want to protect the ones we love and want to have a sense that we can prevent any harm from happening to them.

However, in trials like this, it is a bias that can lead to injustice being done. During deliberations, you might hear your fellow jurors speculating about what my client could have done, but the next question should be, "Is it reasonable to expect anyone could have done that?"

*I am asking you all to not do that—to be fair and to resist that tendency to put yourselves in this situation retroactively and to be a Monday morning quarterback. The instruction that the judge will give to you on comparative fault is that you must decide whether my client's conduct fell below that standard which we might reasonably expect a person to exercise for his/her own safety and protection. The instruction is to determine what is **reasonable** to do, not whether **anything** could have been done or to simply accept the defense's finger-pointing from the person who actually caused this collision.*

You must decide whether the plaintiff was at fault and, if so, to what degree their actions contributed to the injuries suffered. In deciding whether the plaintiff contributed to the injuries sustained, you must determine whether the plaintiff's conduct fell below that standard that we might reasonably expect a person to exercise for his/her own safety and protection, the standard being that of a reasonable person in like circumstances.

The attorney acknowledges our tendency to blame the victim and lets the jury know that they cannot allow that bias to creep into deliberations. The jury instructions include a directive to only consider what a reasonable person should have done to avoid suffering the consequences of the defendant's negligence. If one juror goes into deliberations guarding against the bias and is willing to call it out using the jury's instruction, then you will have succeeded in preparing them to fairly deliberate on the issue. Here's another example. This one incorporates the instruction on the burden of proof:

You must avoid falling into the trap of thinking about all the things my client could have done to avoid the negligence of the defendant. You must only consider what a reasonable person should have done to avoid suffering the consequences of the unexpected negligence of the defendant. No person could ever be held to a standard of doing everything possible to avoid the unexpected. No person could ever be held to a standard of reacting perfectly to the unexpected. It is the law and the standard you must use to consider what is reasonable to do or not do in the circumstances of this case. Remember this instruction…

The defendant has suggested a way that my client caused this collision. They have the burden of proof in proving that my client was negligent and that their negligence was a cause of the crash. We have proved that the defendant caused the collision. When you speed through a red light, it is something no reasonable person would do—it's negligent. What have they presented that proves my client caused the collision? Nothing. The truth is that every accident, every injury ever experienced by people, could have been avoided in retrospect. We want to believe that we could avoid the same awful fate of another person harmed the way my client was. Please resist this tendency and follow the law. Ask your fellow jurors to follow the law and consider only what is reasonable and not everything that's possible.

If you do this, then the evidence you have seen and heard can only lead to the conclusion that my client acted reasonably and should not be blamed in any way for what the defendant did to them. It's not their fault, and the person who caused this to happen should be held responsible. Let's look at the evidence, or lack of evidence, and remember that they have to prove my client was at fault as much as we have proven the defendant speeding through a red light was the cause.

Economic and Noneconomic Damages

Economic damages are easier to prove and should be presented before the more abstract noneconomic damages in your closing. Economic damages are often given as a potential range, and it's vital that you don't short-change your low number and "leave money on the table." At the same time, exaggerating economic damages can hurt your credibility. Attorneys typically underestimate or minimize the economic damages, so if you believe the upper range of economic damages, argue that this number should be the verdict.

You have to explain the methodology used to determine economic damages, incorporating common sense as well as accepted accounting or economic norms. If the defendant's formulation has a meaningful flaw, contrast their methodologies with yours to undermine the defense's credibility. This way, their suggestion becomes an example of their attempts to deceive, minimize, and depreciate the victim and primes your arguments to undercut their response to the noneconomic damages.

When arguing noneconomic damages, here are the key things to keep in mind:

1. Never Apologize- Never appear uncertain about the amount you're asking for. If you find yourself drafting a closing with statements like "I know it seems like a lot of money" or "If you think this is too much money..." then you have to consider what we discussed in the last chapter about resolving your own biases on damages. Closing is when you will most benefit from the hard introspection you performed prior to the start of the trial. Once you have overcome your own obstacles, you are able to communicate damages to the jury during trial and be confident in closing. If you have been successful in earning their trust, the jury may still dismiss your suggested amount, they'll think that *you* believe it's fair, but they may nevertheless disagree with you and favor a lower amount. Even in that case, your number will have credibility with them and will be a factor in their compensation discussions.

2. Damage to Everyday Life- The real value in noneconomic damages emerge when you can describe or show the effects of the damage on your client's everyday life. It helps to mention these everyday damages and pain so that they are not abstract. The patient can't wipe herself. She needs five minutes to get into a car. She can't turn around when someone calls her name.

If you have planned the closing well, you will have time to discuss the damages in the detail required. Select the best details on the way that non-economic damages affect the client as illustrative of the profound effects on the client. Use your flip chart to bring jurors back to especially poignant and emotional moments. The temptation is to rely on the extraordinary things a client has lost. These are important, but remember that the real value in noneconomic damages is their effect on ordinary life. Here's an example from a case involving chronic pain from a botched spinal surgery:

It's hard to communicate how much this pain affects Delores. We all have experienced pain at some time in life. When we feel pain, it affects everything we do and it affects our moods and emotions. If it was severe pain, we can't do anything but think about it and ending it. If it is a dull constant pain, it might not affect what we do until it just wears us down. Pain affects how we relate to people, or if we even want to be around people. This is something Delores experiences to some de-

gree or another every moment of every day. You heard it in the testimony and in her voice. You saw it, and I know that you also felt how this pain is crushing her more and more each day. It's wearing her down. At times it immobilizes her.

When you think about it, there are dozens of decisions we make every day without a second thought that requires Delores to stop and think and consider how much pain it will cause. We get up and use the restroom, we get up and get a drink of water, we hug our children or kiss our spouse when we leave for work, we turn off the alarm and get out of bed – all without much forethought. These are all things that Delores is forced to think about because of the pain. While we may turn around when someone calls our name, they have to think about it and decide whether turning around is worth the pain they will suffer.

Some of the things we take for granted are not really optional. We use the restroom and wipe ourselves clean afterward. It's automatic for us and we do it without much thought or effort. You saw her embarrassment and humiliation at describing how she has to ask someone to clean her when turning and bending is impossibly painful. Every one of us got in and out of a car this morning. So, did Delores, except it took her 5 minutes and a lot of pain to do it. Getting in and out of a car is something we do without much forethought but not Delores. And that calculus of pain is something that affects her decisions to go anywhere outside of her house, adding to her loneliness and isolation. She has lost so much more than her lifestyle. She has lost some dignity, her independence, simple choices as well as the joy of doing things that brought meaning to her life. Remember the testimony...

Just getting by involves pain. Some of the things that make our lives worthwhile and joyful, such as hugging our child or visiting friends mean more pain for Delores. When you will deliberate, consider what you are doing then, whether it's getting some water or shifting in your chair, that this is something that would cause her pain—pain that the defendant inflicted on them and continues to be inflicted on her.

Note Damages Jurors Might Not Consider

Closing is also the time to introduce damages that aren't always obvious or might seem mundane. For instance:

While the chronic pain disorder affects everything that Delores does and has taken the joy away from many of the things they enjoyed in life, that is not the most devastating part of the pain she suffers. We all feel pain at some point in our lives, and we all understand how it can affect us. The one thing that helps to get us *through pain, or any of those tough times, is knowing that it will be over some time. But for Delores, it will never be over. So she can never experience that hope. And it's the loss of that hope that is the most damaging loss anyone can suffer. Delores has no hope that the pain will ever go away, no hope that someday it will end and she can live the life she chooses again. You heard the testimony about that. When we lose hope, it creates suffering that is inconsolable. You heard her psychiatrist talk about the devastating effect of this realization on Delores. The depression. You heard the testimony of her daughter that the only hope Delores has is that the pain won't be worse in the future if her spine deteriorates and she needs more surgeries.*

How much is hope worth? How do you compensate for the loss of hope that you wil never be free of pain?

We call them "the golden years," because our last few years on this earth are the most valuable. Delores survived the Depression and poverty. She educated herself and established a career long before most women of her generation. She married and raised her children while her husband fought and died in WWII. She struggled as a single mom for decades raising two daughters and helping to raise five grandchildren. She survived on hope and she earned the right to live those golden years the way she wanted. But they took that from her and nothing except some measure of justice now can replace what they took.

Delores has no hope that the pain will ever leave her while she is alive. Remember how this woman with such dignity struggled to communicate her anguish during her testimony. I know you felt that anguish. Some of us shed tears and maybe some of you, like me, just tried to keep your composure. It is a life of suffering that only becomes more crushing the more we learn about it. She only has the hope that the pain will not get worse and the hope that you will provide her with a small measure of justice. For this suffering and to help with the suffering that is to come, we think $10 million is fair and reflects the value of her losses due to the pain and the suffering.

This closing communicates the extent and effects of the damage but also the meaning of the damages to the client. After every argument, the attorney cited specific testimony, using the flip chart to bring jurors back emotionally as well as with memory. There is a drip, drip, drip quality of his presentation ending with the amount of monetary compensation as the only relief to the burden.

Note Damages that Resonated with Jurors

During the trial, you'll sense when jurors are particularly moved by someone's testimony or a piece of evidence. In your closing, you'll want to remind them of those moments, supporting their emotional reaction with the evidence itself. Use the meaning of those damages as a platform to propose money amounts. Your storytelling will reach a crescendo, and the money amount you suggest becomes as much a source of relief to the jury. Injustice affects us all, and justice is relief from the effect of injustice. This is not a manipulation, it is the reality of what you are engaged in as a trial lawyer.

Factor in Aging for Noneconomic Damages

Never short-change noneconomic damages. For instance, attorneys often neglect how noneconomic damages change as the plaintiff ages. Traumatic brain injuries cause brains to age at an accelerated rate, leading to earlier and more significant cognitive impairments. Orthopedic injuries cause traumatic arthritis and increasing disability at an earlier age.

Your client's noneconomic damages are likely to be compounded as they age, and this has to figure into their compensation. Jurors will understand this; we all become anxious about the normal ravages of aging, such as aches and pains, arthritis, increasing dependence on others, and social isolation. If you have helped the jury understand that it is not about the amount of money but more about compensation for present and future damages, they will understand why the amount of monetary compensation is more for the future.

Using analogies on money value is a common tactic and can be as counterproductive as often as it is effective. Baseball players' salaries, racehorses, and paintings are popular. These analogies fail when jurors find paying $20,000 a pitch or $200 million for a painting of sunflowers absurd anyway and resent it. Few jurors would say, "Yeah, I would definitely pay $200 million for that painting."

These analogies can be effective if put in the context of confronting the bias on the money value of damages to things we say are invaluable. Analogies are an indication you have not thought enough about how you can concisely argue the damages. It is much more common for a juror to think, "I wouldn't take a million dollars to have that done to me." It is better to be direct in challenging the bias on money amounts. Here is one example from a case involving the suffering of a traumatic brain injury:

If I wasn't required as an attorney to suggest a money amount as compensation for these damages, I'm not sure I would have ever thought about them in terms of monetary value and I'm guessing none of you ever thought of these things in terms of money value either. Some things we would never sell, and some injuries we would never accept in exchange for money. We say our health or our family is invaluable or priceless. It is. But I am required to suggest an amount and I promised you during voir dire I would only suggest an amount that I thought was truly fair.

For Jerry, I have to suggest a money amount to compensate for brain damage. When you damage the brain, you damage more than just tissue, more than just the ability to think and to learn, or more than the ability to control movement or perception. You heard the testimony of the neuropsychologist on how those functions have been impaired by Jerry's brain damage. That damage will never heal and will only worsen as he ages. But Jerry has lost more than his ability to learn or remember, or his ability to control the tremors in his hand. When you damage the brain, you can lose the one thing that makes each of us unique. We lose the mind as we are, the sense of who we are, and what we are. In a sense, the person Jerry was before he was brain damaged by the defendant no longer exists. The person he was before —the person his family and friends knew as a husband, father, and engineer, the person who had hopes and dreams and knew who he was and where he was going—is gone. The people who knew and loved him see the same man, but not the same person. How do we put a money amount of that kind of loss?

Our brain is the most valuable thing we have. It's what makes us who we are. Putting a monetary value on something that precious feels like I'm cheapening our humanity in some way. All I know is what he and his family told you when they testified: they would give everything they had to get that Jerry back. His wife would give every cent she ever had or would earn to have the same husband back.

If I struggled with this issue of placing a monetary value on Jerry's brain, I suspect you will also struggle with this concept of justice. But I trust that you understand that giving no money as compensation for what he suffers and will suffer would be unjust. All you can do is consider what you believe is a fair money amount to compensate him for these injuries and losses. It tests our willingness to act on the values we say are invaluable. I don't envy you, because your decision will be the decision. The way I resolved this conflict in me was to consider who he was and how much he valued his ability to think and learn and be independent.

Based on what his family told me and other evidence on how he was before the injury, I believe $8 million is a fair amount.

Believe in Your Number

How and why you came to the amount for noneconomic damages are less important than communicating your belief in it. No amount of requested damages will hurt your ultimate verdict if the jury believes you firmly believe your request. Avoid anything that suggests you are attempting to manipulate them or negotiate a number. Presenting a range of potential money damages tells jurors you lack certainty, and that will undermine your credibility. Jurors will usually take the lower level of suggested compensation and then use that amount as the ceiling for compromise during deliberations.

Once you've settled on an amount, don't negotiate with yourself. Don't think you read something in the jury during the trial that suggests you should lower your number. You may have a sense of how the jury responded, but in most instances, you really don't know what they were thinking or reacting to at any moment during any testimony. Some reactions are unmistakable (e.g. crying), but others are less certain (e.g. smiling). In any case, it's a mistake to modify your sincere belief in a fair money amount because some jurors frowned during some damage testimony. Base your amount of suggested compensation on what you believe is fair, not whatever limitations you project onto a jury.

If you don't ask for money damages, you won't get anything. It's rare for a jury to compensate more than what was requested. While you can give permission to jurors to come to their own judgment on the money amount, you cannot let them begin deliberations without you suggesting an amount. As long as the amount you suggest is sincere and you explain why then jurors will not hold it against you or the client.

Addressing Multiple Biases

In 2022, I worked on a case with Geoff Fieger involving a newborn who suffered permanent brain damage when a doctor improperly used forceps and a vacuum during a difficult delivery at Mercy Hospital in Iowa City in 2018. Although the mother was healthy and had previously delivered two children without incident, during this delivery, the baby experienced fetal distress from not receiving sufficient oxygen. Instead of performing a C-section, the doctor chose to use forceps and a vacuum to extract the baby, fracturing the child's skull and causing brain damage in the process. The newborn spent nearly two months in intensive care at the University of Iowa Hospitals and Clinics in Iowa City, and by the age of three, he had cerebral palsy, could not walk, and will require twenty-four-hour care for the rest of his life.

The jury found the hospital and the doctor's clinic were equally negligent and awarded ninety-seven point four million dollars to the baby's parents, the largest verdict in the state for a birth trauma case. After a fourteen-day trial, the jury deliberated just ninety minutes before delivering the verdict.

In his closing, Fieger focused on noneconomic damages to the infant. Holding up photos of the bruised and bleeding child, he used the jury instruction on sympathy to give the jury permission to consider the suffering the baby endured:

This is evidence of what they put that baby through. He was bruised, battered, bleeding. Look at the evidence of injuries that we know were painful. The baby could feel that pain—as well as basic emotions from the pain, like fear.

The emotions and the pain the baby felt are not like what we feel. The defendants argue that we can't know how an infant experiences fear, but understanding their fear doesn't depend on the baby reporting it. We can use our common sense.

As adults, we understand WHY we are feeling pain. Understanding why we are in pain doesn't diminish the pain, but it does circumscribe the pain and makes it tolerable. We understand the pain will end at some point.

Newborns don't experience pain and fear like we do. To them, the fear is amplified by confusion about why and how they have pain. To them, the pain will never end. No one can prove to an exact degree, and the baby will never be able to tell us how terrified and hurting he was while the forceps were slowly crushing his skull and the vacuum was pulling him through an impossible space. None of us wants to think about his experience and even now as I talk about it, I feel awful just saying the words and thinking about a baby experiencing this trauma.

I don't mean to offend you or make you feel mortified, but this is what we are forced to talk about in this lawsuit.

The defendants don't deny this agonizing experience. They can't deny the pain or even the emotions of those terrifying minutes when this child was suffering from being battered and crushed and twisted and pulled.

They just deny that he deserves compensation for it.

Later in his closing, Fieger addressed bias about compensation and how to recognize it.

Most of us feel fear. Some of us have experienced terror and most of us have felt lonely. But none of us have felt it the way this baby did—and will for the rest of his life. To use our own experience of that suffering would be wrong because it creates the conditions for an unjust verdict.

The law does not want you to lose your humanity, however. It does not want you to abandon empathy, which means having emotional distance but still understanding how someone else might feel from an experience.

To not compensate this child would be to ignore his humanity and discount him as a person—and we all know he will experience that more than enough from other people in the future. His brain damage will mark him as different, vulnerable to predators, isolated, or alienated. That's why I say we have a moral obligation to justice as well as a legal obligation to compensate this child for his pain and suffering. If you conclude, as you will, that the defendants were negligent and caused his injuries, then you must decide on compensation. And that is where the potential for bias comes in because the defense in this trial depends on you ignoring the evidence and being focused on issues to incite bias.

Fieger went on to deftly discredit the defense's expert witnesses, appealing to jurors' logical reasoning and empowering them again to use their common sense:

The defense is asking you to ignore their own medical records and the medical records of dozens of doctors at the University of Iowa Hospitals and Clinics in Iowa City. The top medical experts in Iowa, who have no interest in the lawsuit, documented the causes of the injuries. The most devastating injury to the baby's brain was inflicted by the mother's doctor, who allowed an emergency to develop and then panicked and botched the emergency. She committed acts of omission and commission. She neglected the baby, causing injury, and then she directly injured the baby through her actions.

You are allowed to use your common sense and experience in life to judge credibility. Outside the courtroom, we say that if it looks like a duck, walks like a duck and quacks like a duck, it's probably a duck. Inside this courtroom, this defendant needs you to ignore what you see and hear— don't look at the duck. The defense wants you to ignore what the defendants themselves wrote down and what dozens of other doctors documented before any lawsuit was filed.

They want you to ignore the medical records and ignore the treating doctors and only trust two highly paid expert witnesses who ignored what the medical records prove. When was the last time a medical expert had to testify on an opinion that ignores the medical records and the testimony of the treating doctors? To agree with the defense, you would have to ignore all of the doctors' records from Iowa Hospital and Mercy Hospital, ignore the evidence of world-renown medical experts using medical records written before any lawsuit, and believe hired experts who had to ignore all that evidence to justify their opinion. We've all heard about frivolous lawsuits; now you can say you have heard a frivolous defense.

Fieger also confronted another bias: the inherent belief we all share that the doctors we trust could betray that trust. He did this by reminding the jury that the mother had given birth twice before without trouble and that the medical records showed there was nothing about her pelvic structure that contributed to the traumatic injuries her baby endured:

There is a natural bias to not believe that the doctors we trust could betray that trust. We want to believe that our doctors are careful, and we need to trust them to be careful. If this doctor can really mess up and hurt a baby, maybe mine could. It's a natural fear and a bias in favor of doctors. It's pretty common, and it's a natural bias you must acknowledge and overcome during deliberations.

In fact, the more terrible the injuries to a baby, the more some juries want to believe it wasn't the doctor's fault. We need to trust and rely on doctors, so the idea that a doctor could do this to a baby is challenging. That's why we talked about this bias during voir dire and you all said you would make a decision based on facts, not emotions and bias.

Then, he confronts the jurors' natural antipathy to attribute monetary value to a victim's pain and suffering.

There is another reason why juries ignore the obvious evidence that a doctor caused terrible damages to a baby: money. It's true. It's all about money. We usually think it's all about money to the person who is suing the doctor, but it's just as true for the doctor or hospital being sued. Do you think that these parents would rather have a healthy, normal child instead of any amount of money? Do you think their child is thinking about money? But you can be sure that this defense is less a pursuit of the truth as it is an attempt at damage control. It is about money at this point because there is no hope that the child they injured will ever overcome his suffering and have a normal life.

The costs of caring for a child injured like this are tremendous. Tens of millions of dollars over his lifetime. Sometimes our bias gets in the way and argues in de-

liberations that it's too much money, or that the parents or the government should take care of the child, instead of the doctor who actually injured the child.

Whenever juries reduce the importance of a case like this to the money, the real meaning of the case is lost. Money is only a symbol of justice. Money will not heal this child. Money is important because it will ease some of the child's pain and suffering and disability. But money will only partly relieve his pain. He will suffer for the rest of his life because of what the defendant did to him. Money will allow people who love him to care for him, but at some point, they will be overwhelmed and exhausted. At some time in the future, they will not be able to care for him. Then either the lives of his siblings will be impacted by what the defendants did to their little brother or it will fall to the people hired to care for him. When jurors think about tens of millions of dollars, they sometimes forget about the child that requires the care he never asked for but deserves.

A fair deliberation begins and ends with what it will take to provide the care this child needs. If the first consideration is what care this child needs and deserves and not some accountant's bottom line, then there is a fair deliberation. If the evidence is that he will need the care, then it would only be just that he gets the money for that care, no matter how much it is or how it might impact the one who is responsible to pay it. If the first consideration is how much money is being requested or how paying this money would affect the defendants, then it is an indication that bias is guiding the deliberation.

Punitive Damages

It never makes sense to ask the jury to punish the defendant with a large verdict, unless punitive damages are allowed by law in the case. It undercuts your argument that compensation is justice for the victim. You can point out the egregiousness of their wrongdoing and the damages their defense has caused, but don't ask for punitive damages. Jurors will factory it in because punishing wrongdoers is as much a reflexive human response as restoring justice is. Trials allowing punitive damages are a rarity anyway and bound for extinction.

When the defense can be accused of hiding evidence, altering documents, perjuring witnesses, denying or minimizing damages, or attacking the plaintiff, bring it up in closing—but only to undermine the defense's credibility rather as an appeal for punishment. Point out the most flagrant or offensive abuses of the defendants as an attempt to cheat the client out of justice, which is in itself damage to the client.

There is a difference between an "honest" defense and a "dirty" defense. An honest defense is based on a fundamental disagreement over facts or blame. A dirty defense relies on falsifying or withholding evidence or accusing the client of "faking" their pain or damages. The latter victimizes your client further, and this should be pointed out to the jury. It's piling fresh damages on top of the original one and should be compensated for. Never argue for punishing defendants to prevent future actions or to may them pay for past actions.

Keep in mind, too, that jurors are more forgiving of lying or deceitful defense tactics. If they spot the same thing on the plaintiff's side, it will be devastating to your case. Fatal. This reflects the bias against plaintiffs who are seeking monetary compensation and another reason why it is critical that you take an honest and open approach to each trial.

Along the same lines, don't take the bait when the defense attacks you. The defense wants to make *you* look defensive, and if you oblige, you'll lose credibility with the jury. Instead, briefly identify the attacks and characterize them as attacks on your client. You're not the one injured here; your client is. Calling out your client's detractors improves your standing with jurors. It is probably more of an advantage to save that issue and argument for rebuttal if it is a part of the defense closing.

Personal Attacks and Rebuttals

While you never want to apologize for the damage amount you request, your closing may be an opportunity to apologize for moments during the trial when your frustration or anger caused you to react in unhelpful ways. Jurors like a spirited contest but they don't like acrimony and personal attacks. That's why we ask our witnesses to never show anger; it causes jurors to recoil from them rather than lean into them.

If you apologized at the time of the outburst, don't bring it back up at closing. But if it was significant enough to be part of the story of the trial- an occasion when you felt that you crossed the line and offended some jurors- briefly acknowledge your regret for that and apologize in your closing. Keep in mind, though, that anger seen as a defense of the client does not offend jurors. That's just you being passionate and authentic. At all costs, avoid fake apologies; they are worse than no apology at all and remove the focus from the client and their case to you. If you have remained authentic during the trial, then the argument on the issues is sufficient.

The rebuttal is the opportunity to get in the last words and emotions and the moment when you can bring the trial to a crescendo. Remember the principle of primacy and recency: the first and last stimuli have disproportionate influence over memory and subsequent behavior. After your first witness, the rebuttal will have the greatest impact on the jury. Rebuttals are the best opportunity to prime the jury's emotions and send them into deliberations with your words ringing in their ears.

It's also a time to be mindful of your emotions. Rebuttal can be rife with anxiety. You are about to relinquish control to the jury. It's like sending your child to school for the first time: you don't want to let them go, but you know you have to and you want to be sure they have everything they might need. If you don't trust the jury, then you might panic and lose focus on the narrative. If you trust the jury and are comfortable relinquishing control, you still can't be certain what the jury will decide. Whatever the source of your anxiety, it is important to use that anxiety to focus and motivate rather than divert your focus into an ineffective potpourri of denials and incoherent responses. The rebuttal must have a theme and remain focused on that theme.

Although a lot is riding on your rebuttal, it's not so much what you say that's important but how you act. After the defense rests, the jurors won't initially be listening to your response. Instead, they are looking at your reaction. Use your emotions to prime the jury, first to dismiss the defense arguments and secondly to help them use their emotions in the service of the damages verdict. Always lead back to damages. You began the trial revealing your authenticity and trust in the jury and now is the time to remind them of that trust and relationship. Share your reaction to the defense closing argument and then why you feel that way.

What should the focus of your rebuttal be? If I've persuaded you of anything thus far, then you know the answer: "damages, damages, damages." Remember, your goal is to motivate the jurors going into deliberations, so select two or three of the most egregious defense arguments, and use specific evidence to rebut them. The defense's misrepresentation of evidence is only an attempt to deceive the jury because the damages are so profound. Their arguments minimizing the injuries or suggesting exaggerations reveal just how staggering a just and fair compensation must be. The numbing parade of high-cost "experts" reflects the fact that they spared no expense to avoid compensating their victim.

While your closing provided concise summaries of evidence on verdicts other than damages and should be motivating, the rebuttal is when real energy is required. That energy is in the emotion you show in defense of your client in response to the defense closing. You want the jury to go into deliberations motivated, energized, perhaps agitated. Rebuttals are the one time when you can use anger and indignation constructively in defense of your client and in response to the defense's "egregious violations" of the truth and common decency. If it's not anger you feel but sadness or embarrassment over the defense's misrepresentations, go with that. Your reaction should be authentic and energetic.

Pick two or three of the most blatant misrepresentations or abuses during the trial, show the evidence to rebut them, and move back to damages. If you are angry, incredulous, or offended, show it now. It's not the time for mocking, sarcasm, and insulting accusations. But if the defendant attacked your client or used degrading language, respond vigorously. Bring it all back to damages.

Other than rebutting the methodologies and evidence on economic damages of the defendants, it's counterproductive to dispute money amounts. If the defense presentation on noneconomic damages attacked your client or their dignity as a human, refocus your own arguments on damages. The defense undoubtedly attacked money amounts in their closing. You can respond without debating the actual amounts by pointing out that money is the issue in every trial. But the money being suggested means something very different to them than it does to you. Money damages mean money the defendants will have to provide, so of course, they believe that what you have suggested (or any amount) is excessive. This is the reason why we are all in court. It is money that will cost them in profits or otherwise, and they want to give as little of what they have as possible.

However, money to the plaintiff means justice. No amount of money will heal all the damages or erase the memory of what the defendant did to them. Money is the only form of justice available to the jury. There is no eye for an eye. There is no punishing the defendants by doing the same to them that they did to your client. Besides, your client wouldn't want anyone else to suffer the way they are suffering. No amount of money will heal or erase the trauma or the wrongdoing they are enduring. Money as compensation is symbolic justice and the amount of monetary compensation is a representation of justice and the values we hold on the worth of what they have suffered.

If plaintiff attorneys are greedy, they are greedy for justice, and they want every penny of justice their client deserves. Money is not the issue; justice is the issue. Money is the tool they are being given by the law to purchase justice for your client. Finally, empower and inspire your champions among the jury. Remind them that creating justice is an opportunity people rarely have, and a kind of healing that affects more than just the victims of injustice. Here are a few more things to keep in mind during closing and rebuttal:

Language in Closing and Rebuttal

Language is important during the trial and especially important in closing arguments and rebuttals. Avoid using the word "award." Your client's not winning the lottery. Avoid legalese and clinical language. Attorneys spend so much time writing and arguing motions and discussing the evidence with other attorneys that they forget how to use plain language that jurors can understand quickly and easily. Your language should be calibrated to communicate effectively with a high school level educated person; even the Ph.Ds. in the jury box will appreciate your clarity and directness. Use your emotions to find your words. "Speaking from the heart" is always more effective.

Use language that evokes emotions as well as concepts. A patient who suffered an injury because they did not receive adequate treatment is "abandoned" or "ignored." A victim of medical malpractice was "betrayed" by the doctor they trusted. A person who suffers pain from burns has "searing" pain. A company guilty of tortious interference "sneaks" and "plots" and "stabs" a partner in the back. Words like terror, horror, crippling, or cheating connote not just the action or effect but also emotions and have a profound impact. Recall the discussion on how the brain perceives and acts on perceptions: persuasion always involves emotions. The language of persuasion is emotional. Don't use inflammatory language that distorts or exaggerates what actually happened; an authentic, honest presentation is more effective.

Warning Jurors

Anticipate points of resistance during deliberations and proactively address them. The defense will nurture red herrings, biases, diversions, and outright obfuscations, so remind (warn) your champions on the jury of pertinent instructions and use examples of defense arguments as violations of oaths and duties. "If you hear another juror mention this or that then remind them of their oath and duty to put aside prejudice…"

This can quickly extinguish unhelpful deliberations early. Allowing a juror to voice a bias normalizes the discussion and can lead to coalitions developing. Empower your champions to nip those in the bud, but do it in a cautious and considerate manner that doesn't single out any juror. Instead, attribute your anxiety about the issue to the defense's attempt to manipulate or deceive jurors. For example:

I think I heard an attempt by the defense to appeal to a certain bias, so I wanted to alert you to this. When the defense told you [this] it wasn't about evidence that is relevant. I think it was an attempt to appeal to the bias because it focuses on the form and not the substance of the evidence. So, if someone suggests during deliberation that you consider this, remind everyone of the oaths you swore and the need to judge the case with real evidence and not prejudice."

Use a light touch. Too strong a warning can come off as defensive and lend more weight to it. You want to discourage the bias without suggesting you don't trust the jurors to be unbiased. Too much attacking of defenses can also seem defensive, personal, and offensive to juries. Still, you want to alert our champions to recognize appeals to bias and give them tools to pre-empt it. "If you hear a fellow juror saying … remind them and everyone that bias cannot be a part of the decision."

Key Takeaways

- When delivering your closing argument, draw from the pool of emotions that motivated you during the months or years of work on the case. Some attorneys tap into their anger and others embrace their compassion for their clients. As long as your emotion is authentic, it will resonate with the jury. Don't let your anxiety dictate your tone; closings rarely sway a jury's verdict but they will empower your champions to fight for you during deliberations.
- Don't cram your closing with too much evidence. Keep it simple. Remind jurors of your strongest evidence—the evidence that most strongly supports your narrative. Explain how this key evidence helps jurors complete the verdict form. Give your champions the tools they need to undercut the adverse jurors' attempts to obfuscate.
- Model deliberations for jurors to help them speed up their deliberations. Show them how to fill out the verdict form, perhaps with an enlarged copy of that form. Present supporting evidence as a concise printed list that defines negligence.
- Connect negligence evidence to damages. Damages, damages, damages. Damages alone won't lead to a negligence verdict but damage evidence re-

inforces the effectiveness of negligence evidence.
- Never overreact to personal attacks from opposing counsel. This will hurt your credibility. Instead, treat the attacks on you as attacks on your client. Defending your client will be seen by jurors as a defense of the jury itself. The jury will support you if you don't get defensive but instead unfailingly advocate for your client.
- Your closing should bring your narrative to the moment where the jury must step in and write the conclusion. Point jurors to the only just ending. Empower them to act. Jurors respond to calls to action when they understand the significance of their role and see an opportunity to help rebuild a suffering person's life or change society for the better.
- Carefully document economic damages and measure the value of noneconomic damages in terms of the effect those damages had on your client's everyday life. They will never sleep more than two hours at a time. They can't clean themselves. Never apologize for the compensation you're seeking and note how damages are often exacerbated as a person ages.
- Your rebuttal will have a big impact on the jury and its subsequent behavior. Focus and motivate. Understand that jurors won't necessarily be listening to what you say in rebuttal but will notice how you react. Dismiss the defense arguments and then compel jurors to use their emotions in service of the damages verdict. Exhibit real energy in defense of your client so jurors enter deliberations motivated to deliver justice.

***

How Should You Decide How Much to Ask for?

Research conducted for academic journals says that if you are too high, your request will be rejected outright. But, on the other hand, if you are too conservative and your request gets discounted by the jury because they assume you're inflating the number, you end up leaving money on the table. The prevailing wisdom is that you want to come in with what is a moderate-to-high amount or moderate-to-low anchor as a starting point.

Should you use focus groups or mock trials to test out different award amounts? The range of damages given by the mock jurors on individual verdict forms can help you decide what an appropriate medium-high anchor would be for a given case. Listening to mock jurors deliberate can also reveal personal anchors or damages formulas that may resonate with jurors in your venue.

Jurors often use their own experiences to evaluate damages. To prevent this and to keep jurors on task, tie damages to the law and what the jury has to figure out. Keep jurors focused on the evidence and the verdict form during your closing. Some attorneys use a whiteboard flip chart so they can visually add up damages during their closing. Show the jury what you want it to decide – don't rely on jurors to reach your desired result on their own.

Assigning financial compensation for damages is a difficult task for jurors. Here's how to make it easier for them:

- Ask jurors to make awards for multiple discrete categories rather than as a lump sum. So, an award for disability/physical impairment, disfigurement, mental anguish, and loss of enjoyment of life. You have to get the judge to agree to this on the verdict form but you can also suggest it in closing.
- When talking about noneconomic damages and what amounts should be awarded, point to specific examples supporting each element of the damages instruction and use the word *evidence* to describe factors in the case that support a damage award for each category of non-economic loss. For example, "You heard the evidence about how Brian can no longer attend his son's baseball games because of his depression." This approach demonstrates that this is an evidence-based decision, not an emotional or arbitrary one.

Ask the jury, *Would it be right to do nothing when a person dies unjustly?* No life is worthless. To do nothing is to support injustice.

***

Chapter Eight:
Trial Research and Final Perspectives

The case involved a woman of Mexican descent who was living in a rural area of southern Illinois when she was T-boned by a UPS truck and seriously injured. Our concern from the start was that the community where the trial would be held- an agricultural town of about 23,000 people- would not be particularly supportive of our case. Farmers typically don't make great plaintiff jurors. (I think this has changed significantly in the last decade. Urban jurors seem to be much more ideological and resistant to changing their minds or biases, whereas rural jurors may tend to be conservative but are much more community-oriented and less inflexible). They are used to hardships. They break a leg, get it set, and that afternoon, they're back out in their fields plowing the back forty. That's the life they live. They live season to season, and they aren't inclined to give out a ton of money to plaintiffs.

In the days leading up to the trial and voir dire, I spent some time in local establishments to try and get a sense of the community. As I sat in one local bar listening to people talk, I heard a lot of complaining about the government. It was too big. It took too much from the working man. It wasn't there to support farmers. Illegal immigrants. Build a wall. About ninety-nine percent of the town voted for Trump in 2016. This, of course, did not bode well for our case representing this Mexican-American woman.

But as I sat and listened and got to know a few of the regulars, something else emerged. As conservative and alienated as the townsfolk sounded, there was also a prevailing sense of community, a sense among the residents that they had to stick together and look out for each other. They had to protect their community against the outside forces. So, we fashioned our voir dire questions to draw out that sentiment. How would you react to knowing that one of your working-class neighbors was seriously injured when an out-of-town delivery truck crumpled her vehicle? Rather than trying to overcome any prevailing political sentiment, we nurtured their sense of community. Our client ended up getting record compensation for that county.

Research helps identify blind spots in your case. After spending so much time on the legal issues in a case, attorneys can develop tunnel vision. Issues we think are significant turn out to be moot and issues we never anticipated become vital. Paradoxically, using a jury consultant and research can be a siren song to losing authenticity. You must have an understanding of consultants and their methods to guard against losing yourself. In a case in Lexington, South Carolina, we represented the estate of an orthopedic surgeon who was killed by his partners after they performed knee replacement surgery on him. (The doctors were motivated to minimize his pain but failed to communicate well and our client died of an anesthesia overdose). It was the summer just after 9/11, and our client, a Muslim, was chief of orthopedic surgery at the medical center, which was the largest employer in the county. How would a jury in the Deep South react to a Muslim family suing the largest employer in the county? We were worried, but when the research came back, we learned that our client was so beloved by his coworkers that we were able to make his faith work in our favor.

In another case- this one involving a dispute over inverse condemnation- a judge ruled that the electrical capacity of a property being taken could be considered as part of the overall value. But he ruled that the plaintiff could not argue that the electrical system was inoperable. We were concerned about the issue until the research demonstrated that electrical capacity was never considered during deliberations. That case demonstrated how good research will reveal and enlighten.

Planning for research can also help an attorney focus and simplify their case. Is the issue being researched more appropriate for a focus group or a mock trial? The answer is in part based on how the attorney is able to articulate it. In one "palimony" trial, the attorneys were concerned about how their client came across to jurors and if it would affect the verdict. That's a focus group-type question. How does a jury decide the issue of comparative negligence in an auto case or compensation in a birth trauma case? Those complex questions are more appropriate for a mock trial. There is no single solution to pretrial research.

The point here is that pretrial research can take many forms and answer questions you may never have asked otherwise. Talking with other attorneys is not research and is often not helpful as it diverts you from being you and your story. You can conduct polls and mock juries, stage focus groups, pore over social media posts, and put together shadow juries. You can hire consultants to study the potential jury pool and even do handwriting analysis on prospective jurors. You can hire people to sit at the plaintiff's table to recommend questions and gauge jurors' reactions. You can even do what I did: sit and listen. Research can improve your chances of success at trial, but it's not guaranteed. So, be a wise consumer. Learn about the available tools and understand their limitations; no consultant or researcher can predict the outcome of every trial.

I have a photograph of me being interviewed by Beth Karas of Court T.V. during the Jenny Jones trial. The family of Scott Amedure, a show guest who revealed his affection for another male guest and was later killed by the man, had sued *The Jenny Jones Show* for wrongful death stemming from the ambush tactics the show used. The jury was deliberating, and Karas wanted me to predict the verdict. I had done a ton of research before and during the trial, but I was not eager to make a prediction. I had no idea what the jury would decide and didn't want to make a fool of myself on national T.V. But Karas pressed me, and finally, I predicted that the jury would find in favor of the plaintiff and set compensation at $25 million.

My prediction was based on gut instinct, but that's exactly what the jury decided. Was it my subconscious? ESP? No, it was a pure guess from a nervous guy worried about looking foolish. There is no magic, and any consultant that guarantees a win is engaging in theatrics or is too narcissistic to be helpful.

If your case is large enough, however, research and consultants can load the dice in your favor. Some consultants also provide attorney coaching, trial graphics, and witness preparation. To gain that edge, though, you must make cost-effectiveness your paramount consideration. Trial consultants have been helping attorneys for decades, and the research methods they use have become more valid and robust over time. They improve your odds of winning, but it is far from an exact science.

As good as the social sciences have become in understanding human behavior, consistently predicting human behavior remains an elusive goal. We understand how people make decisions, but the variables that contribute to that process aren't always clear and are hard to identify. The only safe prediction you can make is that people will surprise you. Those surprises can be a function of some obscure event in their life that would have been impossible to anticipate. Ultimately, the best you can do is to be as thorough as you can within yourself and with your case.

Research Methods

Consultants use a variety of research techniques, including mock trials, focus groups, and polling. Each approach identifies patterns or factors to produce a predictive model. To interpret and use the results effectively, you must be aware of their limitations. As we all learned during the COVID pandemic, models are just a representation of some reality that you hope has predictive value. The more data poured into your model, the better its predictive value.

In trial work, though, getting enough data for a valid sample set is expensive and requires unique expertise. Extrapolating trial outcomes based on a sample of a few participants is precarious, and plausibility depends on a good sample of participants, presenting them with adequate information, collecting the right data, and cautiously interpreting the results. It's a lot of work, and outcomes can be deceiving. Without the proper perspective, negative results from research can be discouraging rather than enlightening.

I approach trial research as I did neuropsychological testing results when I was doing therapy: more data is better and beware of the interpretation. To be a wise consumer you should know the value and the limitations of the research methods and the skill of the consultant doing the research. To use consultants most effectively, you must know the key questions to be researched and which method best delivers answers. For example, a focus group might be the best way to assess the credibility of a specific witness while a mock jury trial might make sense if you face several problem issues in a large case exceeding $1 million. The two most important considerations are: how likely will the research method provide the answers and at what costs? Here are the pros and cons of the primary research tools:

Polling

Polling is expensive because it requires a larger sample to be effective. Also, the polling questions must be carefully constructed; they can't be designed to obtain the desired answer the way political polls do. Your polling questionnaire must be neutral on the issues being polled, and people are needed to interview, collect and analyze the data. This adds to the expense.

Polling is a sledgehammer tool lacking precision. Polling results are most effective in supporting motions to change venue and least effective in predicting trial outcomes. Polling essentially assesses the general public's knowledge and opinions of a case based either on media reports or a description provided by the pollster.

Focus Groups

Focus groups, originally developed by the advertising industry to test reactions to a product or ad campaign, are a good way to assess reactions to a specific trial issue. For example, in one "palimony" case in which there were a lot of "he said-she said" disputes, we recorded our client's deposition. We were concerned that he wasn't likable and lacked credibility. So we carefully selected a group of people to represent a cross-section of likely jurors and had them watch the deposition. We then had focus group members privately fill out a questionnaire before discussing the client's performance and demeanor.

Our fears were affirmed. Overall, the focus group disliked our client. Nevertheless, the women thought he was believable while the men were divided about his credibility. The most valuable takeaway was that all the participants agreed on what made our client less credible, and we were able to mitigate that effect at trial.

Focus groups typically consist of a moderator leading a discussion among six to ten participants. The participants should reflect a cross-section of the potential jury pool. Oversampling one population section—too many retirees, for instance, or far more women than men—will skew the results and make them less predictive. But when a focus group is diverse and reflects the potential jury pool, it can produce a valid and reliable result. All participants reacting similarly is a good indication that the result is valid and reliable. When there is a lot of variability in the results, avoid the temptation to extrapolate from the individual responses. Just because a white male decides differently from a black male doesn't mean all white males will respond the same way.

The quality of the results also relies on having a skillful leader. The group discussion usually lasts a couple of hours and is held at a neutral site that won't unduly affect the responses. Most sessions are recorded, and attorneys and consultants may watch proceedings from a separate room. During the pandemic, many sessions were done via Zoom. This is far less preferable than face-to-face sessions because you can't see nonverbal responses or how group dynamics play out- all key bits of information.

A focus group can reveal general trends in the decisions that will be made at trial, particularly if there is little variability in responses. But variability has value, too; it can provide insights into what factors are influential in the case. For example, a focus group may come to many different decisions in the same case, but if the same facts of evidence are influential in all of these differing decisions, then it suggests a key focus for preparation.

The leader must be a trained and skilled interviewer. They must be familiar with the case, the witnesses, and evidence that might be influential. The interviewer must also understand group dynamics. An untrained leader can lead a group to an undesired end without being aware of it.

Mock Trials

Mock trials generally consist of a one or, two-day long presentation of evidence, arguments, and, at times, witnesses. It is an expensive form of research but can yield the most insight. Mock trials are most useful in complex cases or those with potentially large money verdicts that justify the expense.

Like focus groups, mock juries should represent the potential jury pool. A market research firm can recruit participants using a "screening instrument" questionnaire and a science-based, random-selection method. This screening instrument includes qualifications for participants that must be met, such as being qualified for jury duty. (A list of people called for jury duty in your venue for the past few months will give you a decent outline of the demographics you need.) The questionnaire should also screen out anyone with a connection or possible interest in the case, such as employees of a corporate defendant or a former patient of the defendant in a medical malpractice case. You need enough participants to constitute three juries, each of which will deliberate independently of the other.

Participants must sign confidentiality agreements and fill out a questionnaire on demographics, life experiences, beliefs, and biases. This questionnaire is later used to identify any characteristics that reliably predict favorable and unfavorable jurors. For example, in a case involving an incident with three drivers, the plaintiff was crippled when he was forced off the road during a road rage incident involving two defendants- an uninsured driver with a suspended license and an automotive company executive driving a company vehicle on company business. Each defendant blamed the other defendant, and we wanted to know if jurors would believe the road rage narrative and how they would decide fault in the case.

The questionnaire revealed that when a juror drove more than 10,000 miles a year, they always saw the issue as road rage and apportioned fault equally between defendants. In voir dire, a key question was to ask potential jurors how many miles they drove each year, and the understanding we developed helped us secure a twenty-six million dollar verdict.

In most mock trials, attorneys present a hybrid closing summarizing the key evidence, testimony, and arguments to all three jury pools at once. Jurors then fill out a questionnaire assessing the strength of commitments to the case, most persuasive evidence and arguments, and verdicts are given after each presentation. This approach measures the effectiveness of each presentation and assesses what evidence or arguments work with different types of individuals. No one can predict the composition of the jury pool, but this type of data can help identify which evidence will likely be most effective given the jury selected.

After all attorney presentations and questionnaires are completed, participants are assigned to one of three juries that will deliberate independently. The makeup of those three juries is determined by the questionnaires. One jury consists of the most polarized jurors, evenly divided between jurors most in favor of and most against the plaintiff's case. The second jury consists of the "fence-sitters"- the most neutral jurors entering deliberations. The third group, the "reference jury," provides a reference of results to the other juries. Juries are provided the verdicts form and instructions, told they must be unanimous in their verdicts, and left to deliberate. Their deliberations are observed and recorded. Just as the questionnaires assessed individual decision dynamics, the jury deliberations assess group dynamics.

Dividing the groups as polarized and neutral allows you to see how those dynamics affect deliberations and outcomes. The reference jury provides some guidance if the other two groups have different verdicts. After the verdicts are reached, each jury is debriefed in a focus group-type manner. The least reliable result of this method (or any method) is compensation, but if all three juries arrive at similar results independently, the attorney can develop a more reliable money range for settlement negotiations or for trial.

Mock trials provide enough data to trust the trends and understand likely group dynamics. They can help you select the right people at trial, and which evidence and closing to present based on the actual makeup of the jury. You can develop a strong sense of what jury deliberations will be like and what issues are likely to cause the most discussion so you can tailor your presentation for maximum effectiveness.

Mock trials work best when conducted over a single day. Stretching it to two days results in participants conducting their own research or becoming contaminated in some other way. Even if you lose your case in a mock trial you can come out ahead, knowing what won't work. In the Jenny Jones case, we lost all six research exercises, but along the way, we learned how to win the case.

At-trial Research

At trial, handwriting analysis, shadow juries, and online/background research can also help your case.

Handwriting analysis provides information about individual jurors based on a sample of their handwriting, typically from jury questionnaires from the court. Not all experts like it, but I find it to be a reliable if limited tool. It can help you discern who the introverts and extroverts are, whether they are honest or dishonest and whether they exhibit significant attitudes. You can identify jurors who may be filtering information through a certain lens shaped by life experiences, such as abuse in their childhood. Handwriting analysis is no substitute for having a strong emotional acuity, but it can help solidify those sensations.

Shadow juries are an expensive method during the trial to assess how a jury of like composition is reacting to the trial and proofs. Shadow jurors approximate the demographic and experiences of existing jurors and give you "real-time" feedback on how your case is landing with the actual jury. The results are often dubious and I've never used one for research. Warner Bros used a shadow jury during the Jenny Jones trial but lost anyway.

Advice at Trial

As I've mentioned before, I sit beside the attorney at trial, suggesting questions and offering tactical advice. It's always worked well for me and my attorneys, but this approach is rare. Still, I think my presence allows the attorney to focus on asking questions and listening carefully to answers—key elements of forming a trusting relationship with jurors.

If you want to use this approach, find a consultant willing to develop an intimate knowledge of your case and collaborate with you. The consultant needs to be judicious about their suggestions, never distracting or insistent. The consultant's role is to help focus, expand on testimony, and help the attorney exploit lines of questioning. The attorney is the captain of the ship and the consultant should know where they want to go.

Online and Background Research

I'm not a big fan of conducting social media research on jurors or defense witnesses. It's unethical and unreliable. Facebook posts don't provide any predictive value on the decisions a juror will make at trial, partly because that decision is so influenced by group dynamics. Jurors have been disqualified because of biased comments made on their social media or because they tried to communicate with other jurors through social media. It's true that social media posts can provide background data on jurors and that the more knowledge you can acquire the better, but when forming an opinion of someone, I prefer to trust my instincts. Defenses routinely research and use social media platforms to develop information to prejudice a jury. This happens so much that I always strongly recommend that law firms require plaintiffs to discontinue their social media participation before a lawsuit is filed.

Finding the Right Consultant

Selecting a consultant can be as treacherous as dating on Tinder, or, as Dave Chappelle once said, "Until you are married, you are only dating that person's representative." Take the time to ask other attorneys what their experience was working with them. Take the time to learn about them as you would a new client. Use your gut. Intuition and first impressions are in play as well as your ease in communicating with the consultant. The biggest red flag is the consultant who wants to turn you into them rather than learn about you and bring out that part of you that is waiting to emerge.

No trial consultant has magic or a magic formula. Successful consultants look for the magic in the attorney and bring it out. Attorney Craig Hilborn and I met once at a trial lawyer's seminar where I was speaking. He introduced himself and immediately challenged me. "I don't trust jury consultants," he said, watching my expression carefully.

I smiled. "Good," I said. "Neither do I. If we ever work together, I expect that you would never just take a suggestion without being sure it was the right one for you." We started working together not long after that. Our first case was the retrial of a case that had ended in a hung jury. On the second go-round, Craig won a large verdict. Did his consultant make the difference? Hard to say. All I was doing was helping Craig be a better attorney. I guess the verdict suggests he was. I know my friendship with him afterward has made me a better person.

Avoid consultants who tell you what to do rather than discuss with you what might work best for you. They need to conform their style to yours. Not every consultant is a good researcher and not every researcher is a good consultant; it is a rare consultant who can master both skills. A consultant who tells an attorney what to do and how to do it is probably wrong in their advice but certainly wrong in how they are giving that advice. Beware of jargon, marketing names for techniques, and anyone who has more answers than questions.

I don't want an attorney to be like me. That would not be authentic. My job is to figure out how the attorney sees the world and shape my advice to their mind's view. I am not doing therapy; I'm just trying to do what I suggest they do: be authentic and compassionate and have a single-minded pursuit of winning justice. If the result is a happier and healthier attorney, that's icing on the cake. My goal is to help heal a victim, create justice, and leave the attorney a better attorney and a better person.

I think I am pretty good at what I do, but I think this is because I am not done learning yet. I am at a point in my career where I can choose attorneys to work with, but I never know more than the attorney. As a therapist, I never presumed to think that I made the difference for a patient. I cared about them and translated the technology of changing into concepts they could understand and use. As a consultant, I translate what I have learned from great lawyers and pay attention to the attorney, the client, and the central issue. I like to think that I am walking the talk, but I'm not so sure. And I am not so sure that these are the qualities that matter for a consultant. However, I am sure that an attorney who is authentic will be successful as an attorney and as a human being.

A second important consideration is the consultant's history. There is no current licensing body regulating the requirements, fees, and ethics of consultants, and although associations are beginning to form and regulate the practice, attorneys must rely on resumes and references and an established record of success when choosing consultants. Even then, attorneys should maintain a healthy skepticism of consultants, especially any consultant who appears to know more about your case than you do or "knows" how to win your case. Choose well.

Perspectives

For great trial attorneys, the legal profession is a calling rooted in something human and ancient. It is a calling from prophets and scriptures in every culture manifest in ancient literature such as *Isaiah 1:17*: "Learn to do right. Defend the oppressed. Take up the cause of the fatherless, plead the case of the widow."

When I first started working with very successful trial attorneys, I realized they all share a quality that is more important than any advice I could give them. When I first started working with attorneys like Geoffrey Fieger, Ven Johnson, or Gerry Spence, I was struck by their limitless capacity for denial and determination. No matter what problem emerged, they always seemed to respond with defiance and renewed resolve. No matter how badly we got our behinds kicked in court that day, they couldn't wait to get back to court the next day, and then win the trial.

After going through this process several times, I realized that what I mistakenly concluded was denial was something else- courage. It takes courage to go to trial for a "lost cause" and win, courage to say "no" to insulting settlement offers, and courage to fight through your fear of losing a case. What some mistake for denial or narcissism is courage and the noble willingness to fight for a cause. There are narcissists with defenses that prevent them from seeing a trial accurately. They will pursue a trial for themselves and not for their client. What distinguishes courage from narcissism is that courageous lawyers make decisions for their clients and not their egos, and the result of doing so is success.

Another Cause

What trial lawyers do is incredibly important and becoming more important every day in our country. Our country perpetuates injustice while at the same time creating more justice than any other society in history. Many attorneys approach their profession as a business, and more than any other business today, personal injury law is affected by sociopolitical forces. Our society is being increasingly shaped by authoritarian forces and corrupted by money. It requires billions of dollars to be elected president and hundreds of millions of dollars to be elected to Congress. That money often originates from corporations that have their own interests, and those interests are not the establishment of *"Liberte, Egalite, Fraternite."*

These forces are now focused on the judicial branch of government, the last remaining bastion of individual liberties and justice, and the jury system is their prime target. Trial lawyers are required to defend not just victims of injustice but the justice system itself. We're fighting not only corporate and authoritarian political forces but internal forces, such as the "Federalist Society," that are actively undermining the jury system.

Part of their strategy has been a massive public relations campaign to undermine the reputation of lawyers, the practice of law, and public confidence in the jury system. We see it manifest in every trial where jury pools have already been biased against plaintiffs, plaintiff attorneys, and appellate rulings. Trial attorneys must get actively and publicly involved in educating the public. More is at stake than the business of practicing law; trial lawyers help create a more just society and also a healing service to the powerless, the outcast, and the alienated.

Being a good trial attorney is being honest, trustworthy, genuine, and real. These qualities win at trial and with relationships. Too often, the pressures of earning a living, being away from family, or dealing with the frustrations of practicing law in America dulls this perspective and foster a malignant sense of cynicism in you. So, let me share this perspective as a psychologist participating in the legal process, *What you do in trials is far more important on so many levels than is normally appreciated.* Geoffrey Fieger once observed that society could still function without engineers and doctors but would quickly decompensate into violent anarchy without trial lawyers. I agree.

Printed in the USA
CPSIA information can be obtained
at www.ICGtesting.com
LVHW020332010524
778790LV00001B/271